ALBANIAN GRAMMAR

Nouns and Adjectives

Peter J. Barlow

ALBANIAN GRAMMAR: NOUNS AND ADJECTIVES

by Peter Barlow

Bay Foreign Language Books, Aldington, Kent

© Peter Barlow, 2005

ISBN 1 873722 10 9

First published in January 2005 by:

Bay Foreign Language Books
Unit 3(b) Frith Business Centre. Frith Road. Aldington
Ashford. Kent. TN25 7HJ. England
www.baylanguagebooks.co.uk
sales@baylanguagebooks.co.uk
Tel. +44 (0)1233 720020. Fax. +44 (0)1233 721272
Printed and bound by Antony Rowe Ltd,

FOREWORD

Comparisons, as Mrs. Malaprop observed, "are odorous." Given that Albanian nouns are clearly classifiable, and that the number of forms which each noun can have is small compared to a verb, this book may seem less essential than its companion "Albanian Grammar: Albanian Verbs Explained." However, as outlined in the Introduction and Notes for Readers, there are considerable difficulties in the declension and use of Albanian nouns, particularly in the formation of the plural. Apart from anything else, one vowel ending can represent several different grammatical inflexions, as set out in Part F. These and other features of both nouns and adjectives require "**sistematizim**:" I hope that I have achieved this without creating a straitjacket.

Thank you to Selvije Jashari, to Laura Hajdini, for her advice and unfailing patience, and to my wife Jill, for assisting with the preparation of the text – **me largimin e qipujve**, and to those, too many to name, who have answered my endless questions.

My particular thanks go to Dr. Sedat Kuçi and Dr. Vesel Nuhiu, both of the University of Prishtina, for their time, their support and comments on the draft text, and the masterful **parathënie**.

PETER BARLOW, B.A.
Prishtina, January 2005.

PARATHËNIE

Ky libër, siç e vë në dukje edhe vetë autori në hyrjen e tij, ka për qëllim t'u ndihmojë joshqipfolësve që kanë dije elementare të gjuhës shqipe si t'i zgjidhin vështirësitë në të cilat hasin ata. Siç tregon edhe titulli i gramatikës, libri ka të bëjë me emrat dhe mbiemrat e gjuhës shqipe. Në këtë gramatikë janë përfshirë pjesërisht edhe rregullat e drejtshkrimit si dhe çështjet elementare të fonetikës së gjuhës shqipe. Ajo është marrë edhe me shiptimin e fjalëve, vendin e theksit etj. Aty janë përfshirë edhe çështjet e fjalëformimit të emrave dhe mbiemrave. Natyrisht pjesën dërrmuese të lëndës e përbën analiza e emrave të shqipes. Sëkëndejmi del e qartë se autori ka bërë përpjekje të zgjidhë shumë çështje njëherit në këtë gramatikë të emrave dhe mbiemrave të gjuhës shqipe.

Nga vështrimi i përgjithshëm i kësaj gramatike del në pah se autori iu ka qasur librit në mënyrë origjinale e jo fort konvencionale, duke i shikuar çështjet gramatikore të shqipes me syrin e një joshqipfolësi. Prandaj kjo nuk u ngjan shumë gramatikave traditionale të gjuhës shqipe. Shembujt karakteristikë të trajtave të emrave, po edhe të mbiemrave, i ka nxjerrë nga burimet me shkrim të gjuhës shqipe dhe në këtë mënyrë ia ka shtuar vlerën kësaj gramatike, por e ka shtuar edhe besimin e lexuesve në të.

Libri paraqet një kontribut të mirë. Në të u bëhet një analizë shkencore kategorive të ndryshme të emrave dhe të mbiemrave të gjuhës shqipe.

Kuptohet vetvetiu se autori i ka trajtuar të gjitha kategoritë gramatikore të emrave dhe të mbiemrave të gjuhës shqipe, si të numrit, të gjinisë natyrore dhe gramatikore, të rasave; te mbiemrat iu ka kushtuar shkallës së krahasimit, përputhjes në gjini, numër dhe rasa me numrin që e cilëson. (vijon në faqen 8)

PREFACE

This book, as the author makes clear in his Introduction, aims to help non-Albanian speakers with a basic knowledge of the language to solve the difficulties they encounter. As the title of the Grammar indicates, it makes some mention of the rules of orthography, and of elementary phonetics. It also deals with pronunciation, the position of the stress, etc. The formation of nouns and adjectives is also included. Naturally the analysis of Albanian nouns forms the overwhelming part of the text. From this it can clearly be seen that the author has striven to resolve many questions in the single framework of this grammar of Albanian Nouns and Adjectives.

From a general view of this grammar it becomes evident that the author has approached the book in an original and highly unconventional manner, looking at grammatical issues in Albanian with the eye of a foreigner. Thus this does not resemble many traditional Albanian Grammars. He has taken typical examples of the forms of nouns, and also of adjectives, from written sources in the Albanian language, and in this way has both enhanced the value of this Grammar and enhanced the confidence of its readers in it.

This book is a good contribution. In it a scientific analysis of the various categories of Albanian nouns and adjectives is carried out.

It goes without saying that the author has covered all grammatical categories of Albanian nouns and adjectives – Number, Natural and Grammatical Gender, and case: with adjectives he has covered comparison, and agreement with the noun which it qualifies in Gender, Number and Case.

An obvious feature of this grammar is the many classification groups, dividing such groups via chapters into groups, sub-groups and sub-sub-groups. This has been done with

PARATHËNIE (vijon nga faqja 6)

Një gjë që mund të bie në sy te kjo gramatikë është se ajo përfshin shumë grupe të klasifikimit duke i ndarë ato grupe e rregulla në kaptina, grupe, nëngrupe dhe nënnëngrupe. Kjo punë është bërë me një precizitet pedant. Ky klasifikim i stërholluar e bën librin më shumë si një vepër për analizë shkencore sesa një tekst të mësimit praktik të gjuhës. Mbase qëllimi i caktuar për kategorinë e shfrytëzuesve të tij arsyeton këtë qasje interesante të shtruarjes së lëndës gramatikore në këtë tekst.

Libri ka edhe një bibliografi të përzgjedhur mirë dhe të begatshme, në bazë të cilës është hartuar.

Dr. Sedat Kuçi, docent i gjuhës shqipe në Fakultetin e Filologjisë të Universitetit të Prishtinës

Dr. Vesel Nuhiu, professor i gjuhës angleze në Fakultetin e Filologjisë të Universitetit të Prishtinës

PREFACE (continued)

painstaking accuracy. This highly detailed classification makes the book more of a work of scientific analysis than a practical text for teaching the language. Perhaps the stated aim for this category of user justifies this interesting approach to the presentation of the grammatical material in this text.

The book also has a well-selected and plentiful bibliography, on the basis of which it has been compiled.

Dr. Sedat Kuçi, Lecturer in the Albanian Language in the Philological Faculty of the University of Prishtina

Dr. Vesel Nuhiu, Professor of the English Language in the Philological Faculty of the University of Prishtina

CONTENTS

		Page No
	Foreword	5
	Parathënie (Preface)	6/7
	Contents	9
	Introduction	12
	Notes for readers	14
	Some spelling rules	17
	Final **J**	19
	The Heldreich pine	20
	Noun Declension Groups and Classes	21
	Bibliography	23

PART A   NOUNS

I	Elements and Etymology of the Albanian Noun	25
II	Gender	28
III	Number	35
IV	Case	39
V	Definiteness	41
VI	Citation	47
VII	Neuter Nouns	48
VIII	Declension and Case Formation	50
IX	The First Declension	54
X	The Second Declension	64
XI	The Third Declension	67
XII	The Fourth Declension	74
XIII	Plural Declension: Masculine Nouns	76
XIV	Plural Formation: Masculine Nouns	81
XV	Masculine Nouns: Classes based on Formation of Plural	87
XVI	Plural Declension: Feminine Nouns	136
XVII	Plural Formation Classes: Feminine Nouns	139
XVIII	Articulated Nouns	150
XIX	Substantivised Adjectives	151
XX	Nouns with preposed possessive Adjectives	152

XXI	Compound Nouns	154
XXII	Acronyms and Abbreviations	155
XXIII	Nouns used in Phrasal Verbs	157
XXIV	Gender Shift in Nouns	157
XXV	Stress in Nouns	159
XXVI	Use of Cases	161
XXVII	Prefixes and Antonyms	166
XXVIII	Noun Formation by Suffix 1: Agent Nouns and Nouns of Origin	167
XXIX	Noun Formation by Suffix 2: Inanimate (concrete) Nouns	169
XXX	Noun Formation by Suffix 3: Abstract Nouns	170
XXXI	Noun Formation by Suffix 4: Deverbal Nouns	172
XXXII	Noun Formation by Suffix 5: Diminutives	175
XXXIII	Noun Formation by Suffix 6: Pejoratives	175
XXXIV	Formation of Feminine Counterparts	176
XXXV	Masculine Counterparts	178
XXXVI	Aunts and Uncles	179
XXXVII	Formation of other parts of speech from Nouns	179
XXXVIII	Relationship of Meaning and Form	181
XXXIX	False Friends	183
XL	Days of the Week	183
XLI	Nouns denoting Origin or Residence	184
XLII	Surnames	184
XLIII	Geographical Names	185

PART B	ADJECTIVES	
I	Elements of Adjectives	188
II	Articulated Adjectives	190
III	Unarticulated Adjectives	193
IV	Adjective Declension Tables	195
V	Agreement of Adjectives	202

VI	Comparison of Adjectives	203
VII	Position of Adjectives	204
VIII	Possessive Adjectives	205
IX	Adjectives used predicatively	207
X	Verb-related Adjectives	208
XI	Adjectives formed from Nouns	208
XII	Negation of Adjectives	209
XIII	Colours	210

PART C	CLITICS	
I	General	211
II	Declension Tables	212
III	Use of "Definite" Forms	214

PART D	NUMBERS	217

PART E	PREPOSITIONS AND NOMINAL PHRASES	221

PART F	READY REFERENCE LISTS AND TABLES	
I	Masculine Noun-endings with regular Plural Forms	225
II	Inflectional Vowel Suffixes	229
III	Feminine Nouns with Masculine Declension	231
IV	Masculine Nouns with Feminine Declension	232
V	Selection of "False Friends"	234
VI	Feminine Nouns ending in **-ël**, **-ëll**, **-ën**, **-ër**, **-ërr**, **-ëz**, **-ul**, **-ull**, **-ur** and other consonant endings	236
VII	Masculine Nouns ending in **-ël**, **-ëll**, **-ër**, **-ërr**, **-ëz** **-ul**, **-ull** and **-ur**	240
VIII	Feminine nouns forming plural with **-ë**	248
IX	Prepositions and Cases governed	250
X	Family Tree	252

INTRODUCTION

The aim of this book is to provide the reader who has a basic knowledge of Albanian with the principles governing declension of Albanian nouns and adjectives, and the formation of plurals, to set out the Declensions in tabular form, and to deal with difficulties arising in everyday use. The forms shown are Standard Albanian, with very few exceptions, and the reader should not be surprised on encountering other forms in daily use. Indeed, even making allowances for differences in date, there are inconsistencies between the forms put forward as Standard Albanian in the various publications of the **Instituti i Gjuhësisë dhe i Letërsisë** cited in the Bibliography. The grammatical forms put forward here are deductive rather than prescriptive.

The salient problem with regard to nouns is that while there are Declensions and Declension Groups in the Singular, there is scant connection between these and the plural forms. I have shown connections where possible. The sheer number of irregular formations in certain groups has created undesirably long lists, and made symmetry impossible. A simple page-count shows how masculine plurals dominate as a problem.

By comparison with nouns the declension of adjectives is straightforward.

Considerations of space dictate that syntax, orthography, phonetics and etymology, which are well covered elsewhere, are mentioned here only insofar as they affect morphology.

This book is concerned with morphology, thus the focus is on irregular nouns and adjectives;

consequently the only regular forms to be found will be those listed in the minor Classes, and those used as paradigms and in quotations. As to selection, I prefer to include rather than to omit, even at the risk of being accused of pursuing obscure forms: experience shows that it is unwise to dismiss a word as too obscure: I have encountered a surprisingly high proportion of apparently obscure words in everyday usage.

The criterion for inclusion is generally listing in **Fjalori i shqipes së sotme**. I have, however, in general omitted minor spelling variants, technical expressions related to agriculture and livestock husbandry, as well as words listed in the Oxford Albanian-English Dictionary as archaic or regional.

What is a homonym, and what a different shade of meaning? **Rreth** has several different meanings, and two distinguishable plural forms, but appears as one entry in **Fjalori i shqipes së sotme**, whereas the two meanings of **gjak** are listed as separate entries.

Dictionaries are coy when it comes to listing gender-change. Grammarians seem far from unanimous as to which nouns undergo gender-change. **Gramatika e gjuhës shqipe**, perhaps wisely, does not provide a complete list of nouns forming the plural with **-ra** which change gender, merely stating that this occurs **në shumësin e disa emrave të lëndës me prapashtesën -ra** and also **fshat** and **mall.**

There are no rules as to the formation of nouns and adjectives or to the formation of other parts of speech from nouns and adjectives, only guidelines. The user must always check whether a possible derivative exists, and what its precise meaning may be.

NOTES FOR READERS.

1. The following abbreviations are used throughout:

       ADG   Adjective Declension Group
       CF   Citation Form
       FPG   Feminine Plural Group
       MPG   Masculine Plural Group

2. The following symbols are used throughout:

a. * indicates that the English translation given conveys only part of the meaning, and that the meaning should be checked in a dictionary.

b. ´ indicates the position of the stressed syllable where this is irregular: this is used only where absolutely necessary. When placed over the second of two vowels, it indicates that the stress falls on the second vowel of the diphthong. This accent will only very rarely be found in Albanian texts, although it is often used in Dictionaries and sometimes in Grammars.

c. ø indicates that the English translation given refers to an item of Albanian national costume.

d. Certain other symbols are used in various sections.

3. Terminology and categorisation: Nouns:

a. The singular and plural forms are dealt with separately.

b. The singular forms are classified into the well-established system of four Declensions.

c. Within the Singular Declensions the nouns are broken down into groups by reference to CF stem endings.

d. The Plural Declensions are initially divided by gender (based on the singular form) and then into Groups (MPG and FPG) based on the type of the plural stem.

e. Having thus established the way in which plural forms decline, based on plural stem ending (consonant, double consonant, stressed vowel and unstressed vowel) I then classify the plural stems into Classes, based on the way that the plural form is formed from the singular. The principles of that classification are set out below under the heading Noun Declension Groups and Classes, and in more detail at Sections XIV and XVII.

f. Some nouns may appear or be mentioned in more than one Class.

g. Nouns which change gender are listed under their singular gender.

4. Terminology: Adjectives:

a. The most obvious grouping is between Articulated Adjectives and Unarticulated Adjectives. This difference is both apparent and readily definable, and forms the first basis of categorisation.

b. The various forms of declension are set out in the ADG's, which are both explained and set out in tables. The ADG's do not correspond with the division between Articulated and Unarticulated Adjectives.

5. The term "the Oblique cases" refers to the Genitive, Dative and Ablative cases. I have followed

convention in using the Clitics **i/e** as the indicator for the Genitive Case, but have not used the preposition **prej** to indicate the Ablative forms. Notes on the correct usage of the two variants of the Ablative Plural are at Section IV, Paragraph 5.b.

6. To save space, the singular Declension Tables may show the Dative and Ablative forms as a single entry.

7. Verb Classes and Groups are as defined in "Albanian Grammar: Albanian Verbs Explained".

8. For nouns the Citation Form is the Nominative Singular Indefinite, and for adjectives it is the Masculine Singular, including its preceding Clitic where required.

9. Sometimes two nouns will share the same Citation Form and Plural. Other nouns sharing the same Citation Form may have different plural forms. A few nouns acquire an alternative meaning in the plural, usually differentiated by a different plural form, and sometimes yet more meanings. Nouns sharing a Citation Form are described where necessary as homonyms.

10. The order in which alternative forms are listed does not imply preference.

11. To keep the tables compact, I have kept the translation of each noun quoted as short as possible.

12. While most lists are in (Albanian) alphabetical order, in some instances the listing is based on the final syllable, to illustrate the relevant grammatical point.

SOME SPELLING RULES

1. **Drejtshkrimi i gjuhës shqipe** (TIRANA, 1973) is the authority on Albanian spelling rules.

2. It is important to distinguish between the stem and the ending. By way of example, the **-ak** at the end of **austriak** is a (stressed) suffix, placing it in Class 4, whereas the same two letters at the end of the word **gjak** form part of the word itself.

3. Proper Nouns are spelt with a capital letter, and each element of a proper name (except clitics) will have a capital letter, as in **Kongresi i Manastirit**: *the Congress of Manastir*, and names of political parties, historical events, geographical features and stars and constellations. However in titles of books, plays, etc. only the first word has a capital letter, as in **Qyteti pa reklama**: *The Town Without Advertisements* (novel by Ismail Kadare), **Koha ditore** (but abbreviated to **KD**).

4. Consonants:

a. The nine digraphs **dh, gj, ll, nj, rr, sh, th, xh, zh** are each treated as a single letter for all purposes, including alphabetical listing.

b. Although the letters **g** and **n** may mutate to **gj** and **nj** respectively in the course of declension (or conjugation), such changes do not occur in the formation of the Nominative Singular Definite. Nor do they occur when deverbalised nouns are formed.
Accordingly a noun ending in **-ge** or **-ne** forms the Definite Form with the ending **-ia** (instead of **-ja),** as in **filologe/filologia**: *(female) philologist* and **dibrane/dibrania**: *woman from Dibër*. Similarly a

deverbal noun formed from a verb stem ending in **-n** takes the ending **-ie**, as in **parathënie**: *foreword*.

c. Assimilation between adjoining consonants <u>may</u> occur, i.e. an unvoiced consonant immediately preceding a voiced consonant may become voiced. This is not automatic. The reverse is less common.

5. Vowels and stress:

a. References to nouns stressed on the last syllable will generally include monosyllabic nouns.

b. After **g**, **k** and **h**, **-u** is substituted for **-i** in case endings. Likewise after stressed vowels (except **o**), but with a small number of exceptions.

c. At the end of a word a mute **ë** ending can only follow a syllable containing a stressed vowel, e.g. **rruféné**, and **armíqtë**. Where the preceding vowel is unstressed, the mute **ë**, which formerly was part of the ending, has disappeared.

d. A syllable containing **ë** is not normally stressed, unless it is the sole or last vowel of the stem, as in **zëri** or **gjëra**. Thus in **zëdhënës**, the second syllable is stressed. **Mëllë/mëllënj** and **shpërgënj** follow the pattern of the Declensions or Group to which they belong.

e. Usually the first vowel of a diphthong is stressed: this is always so in the final syllable (except **trotuár** and **huá**). However where the stress is on the second vowel, such as **haír** and **haúz**; this is indicated in this book by an acute accent over the second vowel.

f. In masculine noun declension as in verb conjugation, there are examples of the shift between **ua** and **o**, and between **ye** and **e**. Likewise it is normal for final **a**, **e** and **i** to be followed by a suffix beginning with -**u**. After final (stressed) **o** the suffix is -**i**.

g. Accordingly it is entirely predictable that most masculine nouns with stressed final syllables ending in a vowel should belong to the Second Declension, and that nouns such as **hero** should belong to the First Declension.

h. Those masculine nouns ending in stressed **a** which, contrary to the above, take endings beginning with -**i** belong to Group 4 of the First Declension and are all of Turkish origin.

FINAL J

1. Final -**j** modifies the preceding vowel and is pronounced, but does not alter the stress. Compare the pronunciation of **be** and **bej**. Accordingly nouns ending in -**j** in the singular (except **bej** and the name **Skënderbej**) belong to the First Declension.

2. Nouns with a plural stem ending in an unstressed vowel + **j**, such as **popuj** (and all other masculine polysyllabics ending in -**ull**), or in a diphthong + **j**, such as **zhguaj** or **qiej**, where the stress is on the first vowel of the diphthong, belong to MPG 2, and form the Definite plural with -**t** (since final -**ë** cannot follow an unstressed syllable).

3. **Muaj**: *month* (plural **muaj**) takes normal First Declension endings in the singular but in the plural belongs to MPG 2, for the reason set out above. Other nouns with CF in -**j** form the plural with suffixes.

4. All other nouns with plural stems ending in vowel + **j** are either monosyllabic or stressed on the final syllable, as in **kufij**: these nouns can therefore be considered as belonging to MPG 3, or MPG 5. The point is academic, since these groups decline identically.

5. More detail as to proper nouns generally, including those ending in -**j**, is in Section V Paragraphs 18-19:

a. For surnames see Section XLII.

b. For geographical names see Section XLIII.

THE HELDREICH PINE

The reader will find three references to this species in the book, as it has three different names in Albanian. It takes its name from a German aristocrat, Ritter Theodor von Heldreich, born Dresden 1822, died Athens 1902. He spent much of his adult life as Director of the Botanical Gardens in Athens, and additionally classified over 700 species of flora throughout Greece, the Greek islands, and the surrounding area.

NOUN DECLENSION GROUPS AND CLASSES

1. The singular Declensions comprise Groups as follows:

Group	First Declension	Second Declension	Third Declension	Fourth Declension
1	Consonant ending	Endings -g -h -k	Endings -ul -ull -ur	Consonant ending
2	-ël, -ër etc.	None	-ël, -ër etc.	None
3	-ë	None	-ë	-ë
4	Stressed vowel ending	Stressed vowel ending + **bej**	Stressed -i	None
5	Stressed vowel + extension	None	Stressed vowel + extension	None
6	**-ua**	None	**-ua**	None
7	None	**krye**	Unstressed vowel	**krye**
8	None	None	**-ie** and **-je**	None
9	Substantivised adjectives			

2. The plural Declensions comprise Groups as follows:

Group	Masculine (MPG)	Feminine (FPG)
1	Ending in **-ë**	As for masculine
2	Ending in unstressed vowel, **-uj**, **-uaj**, **-iej** and **-yej**	As for masculine
3	Ending in stressed vowel, or stressed vowel + **j**	As for masculine
4	Ending in **-l**, **-r**, **-s**, **-z**	Irregular
5	Ending in other single consonant (not **-t** or **-j**)	As for masculine
6	Ending in double consonant	None
7	**Herc** and other units, also **-t**	**natë**
8	Substantivised adjectives	

3. The Classes based on the way in which the plural is formed are as follows:

Class (M)	Suffix or other change	Class (F)
1	Identical to singular	As masculine
2	Stem vowel change	As masculine
3	-ll and -k change to -j, or, with gender shift, to -je	None
4	Almost all -ë	None
5	Mostly -ë	None
6	-ë for animates, -e + gender shift for inanimates	None
7	-ë for animates, -a for inanimates	None
8	-e causing gender shift	None
9	Singular in -am	None
10	Endings in -ël, -ër -ul -ull -ur followed by -a	As masculine
11	Singular ending in unstressed -ë	As masculine
12	Stressed vowel + -nj	Only **drunj**
13	-nj added to various endings	None
14	**-ër**	None
15	-(ë)ra, sometimes with gender shift	-(ë)ra
16	**-llarë, -lerë**	None
17	Alternative endings	As masculine
(18)	Irregular	Irregular
(19)	Suppletive	**dhen**

Masculine nouns ending in -ë are placed in Class 11 as a clearing-house and have a variety of plural endings. Feminine nouns with this CF ending mostly belong to Class 11 F and form the plural with -a, except for the 106 nouns listed at Part F Section VIII.

BIBLIOGRAPHY

1. Publications of **Instituti i Gjuhësisë dhe Letërsisë i Akademisë së Shkencave të Shqipërisë**

   Drejtshkrimi i gjuhës shqipe (Tirana 1973)

   Fjalori i emrave gjeografikë të Republikës së Shqipërisë (Tirana 2002)

   Fjalori i shqipes së sotme (abbreviated to **Fjalor sh.s.**) (Tirana 2002)

   Gramatika e gjuhës shqipe (Tirana 2002)

   Gramatikë historike e gjuhës shqipe by Profesor Shaban Demiraj (Tirana 2002)

2. Publications of **Enti i Teksteve dhe i Mjeteve Mësimore i Kosovës**

   Gramatika e gjuhës së sotme letrare shqipe (Prishtina 1989)

   Gramatika e gjuhës së sotme shqipe për shkollat e mesme, by Dr. Latif Mulaku and Mr. Ahmet Kelmendi (Prishtina 2002)

   Gjuha letrare shqipe (Prishtina 1984)

   Praktikumi i gjuhës së sotme letrare shqipe by Mr. Fadil Sulejmani (Prishtina 1984)

3. Publications of University Faculties

   Oxford Albanian-English Dictionary by Leonard Newmark (Oxford 1999)

Sistemi i lakimit në gjuhën shqipe by Profesor Shaban Demiraj (Tirana 1973)

Standard Albanian, by Newmark, Hubbard and Prifti (Stanford 1982)

4. Other works

Colloquial Albanian, by Isa Zymberi (Routledge, London, 1991)

El Albanés, by Manuel Sanz Ledesma (Madrid 1996)

Fjalori shqip-anglisht, by Pavli Qesku (Tirana 2000)

Fjalori shqip-gjermanisht, by Olimbi Vito (Tirana 1996)

Albanian Grammar: Albanian Verbs Explained, by P. J. Barlow (Aldington 2002)

5. Quotations

a. Phrases cited from Press sources have been taken from the Daily Press during 2003/4.

b. A few phrases have been taken from the compilation of monograms published under the title **Toponimia e Gjakovës me rrethinë**. These are indicated by the letters **T.Gj.rr.** and not attributed to the individual authors.

c. Quotations from literary works are acknowledged in the usual way.

PART A

NOUNS

I **ELEMENTS AND ETYMOLOGY OF THE ALBANIAN NOUN**

1. The Albanian noun has the normal characteristics of Gender, Number and Case. It has a further, and unusual, characteristic, in that the concept of definiteness is indicated by endings: the Definite Article as such does not exist. Separate sub-declensions, known as Definite and Indefinite Forms, indicate "Definiteness" and "Indefiniteness."

2. It is customary to use the Nominative Singular of the Indefinite Form as the Citation Form. However, given that the gender of certain nouns is not apparent from the ending of the Citation Form, and that the plural can be formed in a variety of ways, the student is advised to learn the following parts of each noun:

   Nominative Singular Indefinite, Nominative Singular Definite and Nominative Plural Indefinite.

3. Although the rules for forming the (Indefinite) Plural are complex, (see Sections XIII-XVII) the Definite Plural, with a handful of exceptions, is formed from this in accordance with straightforward rules.

4. There are four principal Declensions; of these the first two comprise masculine nouns, while feminine nouns follow the patterns of the Third Declension, and neuter nouns make up the Fourth Declension. The plural endings vary according to the plural stem of the noun,

and connections between the singular Declensions and the endings added in the plural are few. Some nouns denoting male beings decline according to the pattern of the Third Declension.

5. Apart from Gerunds and a small number of nouns formed from adjectives and participles, and **krye**: *head*, nouns in Albanian are grammatically masculine or feminine. A few masculine nouns (mostly ending in -**ë**) have vestigial neuter forms.

6. An unusual feature of Albanian noun declension is that certain categories of noun change gender, i.e. become grammatically feminine, on becoming plural. These are principally masculine nouns forming the plural with -**e**, most of which are abstract, but including some inanimate nouns and a few animate nouns. Also some masculine nouns forming the plural with -**ra** (mostly formerly neuter) and all neuter nouns except **krye** become feminine. **Krye** becomes masculine in the plural. Section XXIV has more detail.

7. The plural is formed in a variety of ways, which have no direct connection with the declensions. Generally the formation of the plural depends on the ending of the Nominative Singular Indefinite (the Citation Form), the gender of the noun, and in some instances whether the noun is inanimate or animate. The declension of the plural forms is determined by the ending of the plural stem, without regard to gender, and only with the two (irregular) nouns in FPG 4 is there any difference between the two genders with regard to plural formation.

8. Nouns may also be classified by meaning, i.e. as proper nouns or common nouns, as animate or

inanimate, as abstract or concrete and as collective nouns and nouns denoting substances. These distinctions may be relevant in relation to the formation of the plural, and sometimes in relation to gender-shift. These distinctions are mentioned as they arise, and at Sections XV, XVII, XXIV and XXVIII. A common noun may be used as a proper noun, as in **Mimozë**: *mimosa*, **Shpresë**: *hope*, **Besim**: *trust*, or vice versa as in **lekë** (currency), **xhaul**: *joule*.

9. Compound nouns almost invariably decline in the same way as their second or final element, except for certain units of measurement such as **kale-fuqi**: *horsepower*, and certain compounds of **peshk**: *fish* with **peshk** as their first element.

10. As to etymology, Albanian has drawn its vocabulary from many sources, and with some morphological consequences. Etymological factors primarily affect declension forms, but may affect gender.

11. Turkish origin is reflected in declension, as in:

a. First Declension nouns ending in **á**, e.g. **baba**: *father* (plural **baballarë**) and **budalla**: *fool* (**budallenj**).

b. Second Declension nouns ending in **-í** and forming the plural with **-lerë**, such as **haxhi**: *hajji*.

c. Second Declension Nouns ending in **-çí** or **-xhí** such as **sahatçi**: *watchmaker*.

d. Second Declension nouns ending in **-ëk** such as **matrapazllëk**: *wheeling and dealing*.

e. Third Declension masculine nouns, e.g. **dajë**: *uncle*.

f. Suffixes used to form female counterparts, as in Section XXXIV 6.

12. Many other nouns of Turkish origin decline normally, e.g. **sahat**: *watch, clock*, **allishverish**: *dealings*.

13. The connection between the gender of some nouns ending in **-ull** and the gender of the Latin noun from which they derive is discussed at II 13 c below.

14. The plural of nouns ending in **-gram** depends on their origin: see XV 9 a.

II **GENDER**

1. Grammatically Albanian nouns are almost exclusively masculine or feminine. There is a small number of neuter nouns, which are dealt with elsewhere. It therefore follows that most inanimate objects and abstract ideas which in English are neuter are designated in Albanian by nouns which are masculine or feminine. The gender of such nouns is ascertainable from their form, both from the stem ending (as seen in the CF) and from any inflectional ending, or from any particles or adjectives which define them. A small number of endings is common to both (or in three instances all three) genders.

2. The gender of an animate noun will be determined by its meaning in almost all cases. Thus **shkrimtar** (*male*) *writer* is masculine and belongs to the First Declension while **shkrimtare** (*female*) *writer* is feminine and belongs to the Third Declension. Nouns such as **axhë**: *uncle* (*on father's side*), **gegë**: *Gheg*, **hoxhë**: *holy man* and **toskë**: *Tosk* which belong to the

Third Declension are grammatically masculine, despite their form, and any qualifying adjectives or pronouns will be masculine. Similarly Proper Nouns denoting males such as **Kolë**, **Lekë** and **Ramë** are masculine grammatically, but belong to the Third Declension, while Proper Nouns denoting females and ending in a consonant, such as **Antigon,** belong to the First Declension. Where the gender of an animal has no economic or social significance, such as **mi**: *mouse* and **baldosë**: *badger*, one form may denote both male and female of the species.

3. Usually the ending of the Citation Form of a noun will indicate its grammatical gender. As a general rule nouns ending in a consonant are masculine, whereas those which end in a vowel are feminine. However there are both groups of nouns and individual nouns which are exceptions to this rule. The groups are set out below. In those instances the Nominative of the Definite Form will indicate the gender of the noun.

4. Certain endings, such as -**ë**, -**ël**, -**ër** and -**ull**, are common to masculine and feminine genders; the ending of the Definite Form will indicate the gender of the noun. See Part F for lists of the more common nouns ending in -**ël**, -**ër** and -**ull**.

5. Exceptions to the general rules below are listed individually.

6. Masculine nouns comprise the following categories (all references are to the Citation Form):

a. All nouns ending in a consonant, except for:

i. A significant number ending in -**ël**, -**ër**, -**ull** and -**ur**. See Part F for lists.

ii. A small number with stems ending in -**ëm**, -**ën**, -**ërr**, -**ëz**, -**ul** and a very few others: see Part F and also the notes below the Declension Tables.

iii. Feminine and neuter gerunds formed from participles such as **e shtruar**: *bedding* and **të ecur**: *walking*: other nouns formed from participles such as **i dërguar**: *envoy* will vary according to the gender of the subject. **Trotuár**: *pavement* is also masculine.

b. The following categories of nouns with stems ending in a vowel:

i. All nouns ending in a stressed vowel (including monosyllabics) which extend the stem with -**r** or -**n** in the Oblique cases of the Indefinite Form and in the entire Definite Form. Examples are: **bri**: *horn*, **dru**: *wood*, **dry**: *padlock and* **zë**: *voice*.

ii. Animate nouns with a stressed vowel ending which denote males, such as **baba**: *father*, **ka**: *ox*, **njeri**: *person*, **thi**: *boar* and **vëlla**: *brother*. **Mi**: *mouse* denotes the mouse species rather than a specifically male mouse. Also the following: **atdhe**: *fatherland*, **dhe**: *earth*, **shi**: *rain* and **veri**: *North*. **Njeri**: *person*, although grammatically masculine, can be used to mean a human being of either sex. Most of these belong to the Second Declension.

iii. Nouns ending in -**ua**, except **grua**: *woman, wife* and **hua**: *loan*.

iv. Three groups of nouns ending in -**ë**:

aa. **atë**: *father*, **burrë**: *man, husband*, **djalë**: *boy, son*, **gjumë**: *sleep*, **kalë**: *horse*, **lëmë**: *workyard**, **lumë**: *river*.

bb. Nouns which were formerly neuter, many of which denote substances:

ballë: *forehead*, **brumë**: *dough*, **djathë**: *cheese*, **drithë**: *grain*, **dyllë**: *wax*, **dhallë**: *buttermilk*, **dhjamë**: *grease*, **grurë**: *wheat*, **gjalpë**: *butter*, **mjaltë**: *honey*, **ujë**: *water*.

cc. Nouns ending in -**ë** which denote males but belong to the Third (Feminine) Declension, some of which are listed at Section XI 4 d. Such nouns take masculine agreement, as: **Duka i Madh**: *the Grand Duke*.

7. The following types of noun are feminine:

a. With unstressed vowel endings:

i. Nouns ending in an unstressed -**ë**, except for those listed as masculine, and a small number of neuter nouns, mostly gerunds or formed from adjectives, and therefore articulated.

ii. All nouns ending in unstressed -**e** and unstressed -**o**, such as **lule**: *flower* and **radio**: *radio*, with very few exceptions. Masculine (Third Declension) nouns with these endings include **qole**: *servile person* and **qose**: *man without facial hair*, and a few nouns denoting males and ending in unstressed -**o**, such as **kuqo**: *redhead* and **dhëmbo**: *person with prominent teeth*.

iii. **Grua** and **hua**.

b. With stressed vowel endings:

Nouns ending in stressed -**a**, -**e**, -**ë**, -**i**, -**o**, -**u** and -**y**, except for those animate nouns denoting males, and those nouns which extend the stem with -**r** or -**n** in the singular. This group includes many abstract nouns ending in **-i**, **-ri** and **-si**. Most monosyllabics ending in a vowel are masculine, but the following are feminine:

Fe: *religion*, **pre** : *prey*, **re**: *cloud*, **e re**: *young woman*, **e ve**: *widow*, **dhi**: *nanny goat*, **fli**: *Kosovar pastry dish*, **li**: *smallpox*, **zi**: *mourning* **gjë**: *thing*, and **dru**: *firewood*, musical notes such as **fa** and letters of the alphabet such as **A-ja**, **Zh-ja**.

c. With stems ending in a consonant:

i. Gerunds (other than neuter gerunds) formed from participles, such as **e shpuar**: *stab* and **e ecur**: *gait*.

ii. Nouns ending in **-ël**, **-ëm**, **-ën**, **-ër**, **-ërr**, **-ul**, **-ull** and **-ur** as listed at Part F. Other nouns with these endings (except Gerunds ending in **-ur**) are masculine.

iii. Nouns ending in **-ëz** (with a very few exceptions).

8. Neuter nouns have the following CF endings:

a. Those formed from adjectives mostly end in **-ë**. A few adjectives form neuter nouns without suffix, such as **të ri**: *youth*, **të kuq**: *red, redness* and **të errët**: *darkness*.

b. **Ballë,** which is almost always masculine, and very rarely neuter, and substance nouns as listed at VII 7 a. (also generally declined as masculine nouns in present-day Albanian) likewise end in **-ë**.

c. A small number of substance nouns with consonant endings, as listed in Section VII 7 b. These are also rarely found as neuter nouns in modern Albanian

d. Gerunds retain the ending of the participle from which they are formed.

e. **Krye**: *head*.

9. Acronyms and nouns formed from abbreviations have specific rules for determining their gender, which are set out in Section XXII.

10. When referring to an idea such as a previous sentence, Albanian speakers use the feminine gender, as in:

    Ajo që Diellën e frikësoi edhe më tepër: *that which frightened Djella even more*(Rexhep Zogaj, **Mëkati i Djellës**).

11. Albanian has the phenomenon of **dygjinshmëri**: literally *dual gender*. This term is used to describe those nouns which are of one gender in the singular, and of another gender when plural. This is discussed in more detail in Section XXIV. The nouns in question are: all masculine nouns which form the plural with the suffix **-e**, a number of substance nouns which form the plural with **-ra**, **fshat** (see Section XXIV) and **mall**, and those neuter nouns which have plural forms. These nouns are then qualified by adjectives, demonstratives etc. in the feminine form:

    Toponimet janë përmendore të kulturës së një populli: *place names are memorials of a people's culture*. **T.Gj.rr.**

    Zakonet e çuditshme: *surprising customs*, **mallra të doganuara**: *duty-paid goods*.

12. As to nouns ending in **-ël**, **-ëll**, **-ër**, **-ërr**, **-ull** and **-ur**, there is no simple rule for determining the gender.

Some grammarians point out that the gender can be ascertained from the ending of the Definite Form, which is true if you know this ending already! Equally the gender can often be determined from adjectives in agreement or following Genitives. These nouns illustrate the need to learn, in addition to the Citation Form, the Definite Form and the plural. The lists of nouns with these endings in Part F may assist.

13.a. Most nouns ending in **-ër** are feminine, but the following categories are masculine**:**

i. The units of measurement **metër** and **litër** and their multiples and subdivisions.

ii. Agent nouns, such as **gjeometër**: *surveyor*.

iii. Others as listed at Part F.

b. Many English nouns ending in *-er* have direct counterparts in Albanian, some ending in **-ër**, but many of which end in **-er**.

c. i. Nouns ending in **-ull** derived from Latin nouns which (in Latin) are masculine or neuter (and therefore end in *-us* and *-um* respectively*)*, such as **dishepull**: *disciple* (from *discipulus*) and **tempull**: *temple* (from *templum*) are generally masculine.

ii. Nouns ending in **-ull** derived from Latin nouns which are feminine (and therefore end in *-a*) will generally be feminine. Knowledge of Latin is not always necessary to establish this, as in **shpatull**: *shoulder blade*, where the Latin word *spatula* is found in English. **Pjergull**: *pergola* is an identifiable derivation, although the original Latin word was *pergula*. **Ishull**: *island*, derived from *insula*, is an exception to this proposition, being masculine in Albanian.

14. **Vjehërr**: *father-in-law* and **thjeshtër**: *stepson* decline as masculine nouns, while **vjehërr**: *mother-in-law* and **thjeshtër**: *stepdaughter* have feminine declension. Likewise, but with divergent meanings, **shemër**: *rival* is masculine, and **shemër**: *second wife* is feminine.

15. A few inanimate nouns share a Citation Form with a noun of a different gender. In some instances the meanings are related. In the examples below I deliberately do not list meanings: for the precise differences check in a large dictionary. Examples are:

    dru, **gjeni**, **gjë**, **rregull**, **shpat** and **tëmbël**.

16. Compound units of measurement such as **kalë-fuqi**: *horsepower* and **vit-dritë**: *light-year* take their gender from the first element; only the first element declines.

III NUMBER

1. Albanian nouns have two numbers, singular and plural. Most nouns can be used either in the singular or in the plural. The plural is most frequently formed by the addition of a suffix, but significant numbers of nouns form the plural by changes to the stem vowel, the final stem consonant, or both, in some instances with a suffix, in some without. See Sections XIII to XVII for details.

2. Certain nouns have only singular forms. These are usually nouns indicating abstract concepts. However certain abstract nouns can also be used in the plural.

These include nouns which have acquired a transferred meaning which logically permits this, such as **mbledhje**: *meeting*.

3. The extent to which Gerunds and other deverbal nouns can be used in the plural depends on their meaning, i.e. whether the action described can be repeated or varied.

4. Nouns which can have only singular forms include most abstract nouns, substance nouns (except as set out below), collective nouns (e.g. **pleqëri**: *the old folk, the older generation*), points of the compass and many meteorological phenomena. Some nouns ending in -**i** such as **risi**: *youth* have only a singular form, whereas **risi**: *novelty* has both singular and plural forms.

5. The traditional names of some illnesses, both human and animal, are found only in the singular; others are found only in the plural. Examples are:

    Singular: **fruth**: *measles*, **li**: *smallpox*, **zgjebe**: *scabies*. Plural: **shyta**: *mumps*, **ethe**: *fever*.

    Medical names for illnesses will generally be in the singular, as for example **sinusit**: *sinusitis*.

6. Nouns denoting substances may be used in the plural, when they acquire the meaning "*types of*", e.g.

    gjashtë djathëra: *six (types of) cheese*.

7. Substance nouns may also be used in the plural where the substance in question is normally supplied in a container or a known quantity, e.g.

    dy birra: *two glasses* (or *bottles*) *of beer*.

8. Nouns denoting metals have a change of meaning in the plural:

    argjende/ergjende   *silverware*
    bakëre/bakra   *copper goods*
    hekura   *iron goods*
    plumba   *bullets, lead seals* (for racing cars, meters, etc.)

9. The plural of substance nouns may also be used to indicate a large quantity, as in **10,000 metër kub dhera**: *10,000 m³ of soil* and **të rrethuar nga ujërat e lumit Shkumbin**: *engulfed in the waters of the river Shkumbin* (**Gazeta shqiptare**).

10. While as a general rule collective nouns may be used only in the singular, the following may be used in the plural:

    fis: *clan*, **popull**: *nation, people*, **tufë**: *crowd, flock* and **kope**: *flock, herd*.

11. Some other nouns have only plural forms. These are generally nouns which denote objects not found singly, such as **syze**: *spectacles*, **pinca**: *pliers*. To refer to a single item, or a specific or unspecified number of objects the word **palë**: *pair* is used, as in:

    tri palë zgjedhje: *three sets of elections*, **një palë syzë**: *a pair of spectacles*, **disa palë pantallona**: *some pairs of trousers*.

12. Some nouns formed from participles are found only in the plural:

    të ardhura: *income*, **të fshira**: *sweepings*.

13. Other groups of nouns found only in the plural are:

a. Items consisting of two or more parts, such as **benevrekë**: *white trousers* (ø) and **pantallona**: *trousers*.

b. Groups of animals such as: **dhen**: *flock of sheep* and **shqerra**: *flock of lambs*.

c. **Veta**: *people*, although a singular form (**vetë**) exists.

d. Actions such as: **lajka**: *flatteries*, **teka**: *whims*, **pace**: *insulting gestures*, **gjepura**: *falsehoods*, **të palara**: *dirty deeds*, **vome**: *laments*.

e. Illnesses such as: **ethe**: *fever*, **grykë**: *tonsillitis*.

f. Games such as: **kupa**: *hearts*, **pllaka**: *tag*.

g. The results of activity, e.g.: **të vona**: *late crops*, **të korra**: *harvest*, **të lashta**: *crops*.

h. Various substances, e.g.: **hime**: *bran*, **qurra**: *snot*.

i. Locations such as: **Alpet**: *the Alps*.

j. Religious observances such as: **të lidhura**: *Lent*.

14. Albanian speakers and writers often use collective nouns such as **vajzëria**: *the young girls*, **pleqëri**: *old folk*, **qytetaria**: *the townsfolk*. Also **shtazëri**: *animals*.

15. Generally a noun will be followed by a verb which has the same number, i.e. a singular noun will be followed by a singular verb. In speech, however, and sometimes in writing, a singular collective noun in the Definite Form such as **fëmija**: *the children*, **pleqëria**:

the old folk, **shumësia**: *the majority* or **bota**: *the world* (i.e. everybody) may be followed by a plural verb, as:

"**gjithë shoqëria e tyre rrinin në tarracën e hotelit të madh**" (Ismail Kadare, **Gjenerali i ushtrisë së vdekur.**)

16. Albanian has a number of nouns which are homonyms in the singular but which have different plural forms for the different meanings. Examples are **bar** and **ton** (both Class 5) and **rreth** (Class 17), as well as a few feminine nouns ending in -ë.

17. A few nouns, such as **vit**: *year* and the feminine nouns listed in Class 17F, have a single meaning in the singular but different plural forms to represent different aspects of the meaning.

18. Proper names are rarely found in the plural, but when used in the plural decline normally, as in:

në lagjen e Jasharëve: *in the area where the Jashari family lives*.

Në komunën e Dardanës ka dy Karaçeva, Karaçeva e Epërme dhe Karaçeva e Poshtme: *in the Dardanë municipality there are two Karaçevas, Upper and Lower*.

IV **CASE**

1. Albanian Nouns have the following five cases:

   Nominative, Accusative, Genitive, Dative & Ablative.

2. The functions of the cases are set out in Section XXVI.

3. Singular Declensions are set out in Sections IX-XII: Plural Declensions are set out in Sections XIII and XVI.

4. In the Indefinite Form the Nominative and Accusative are identical, except for articulated nouns (those preceded by an Adjectival Clitic).

5. The Indefinite Form Genitive, Dative and Ablative forms are identical, as they are in the Definite Form, except that:

a. The Genitive is always preceded by a Clitic.

b. The Ablative plural of the Indefinite Form may end in either **-ve** or **-sh**.

i. The original **-sh** ending should be used after cardinal numbers, after indefinite pronouns denoting quantity such as **disa**, and after expressions of quantity such as **shumicë**. After demonstrative pronouns such as **këtyre** and **atyre** the -ve ending should be used.

Examples: **një florë prej 960 llojesh**: *960 plant varieties* (referring to the proposed Kosova National park in the **Bjeshket e Nemuna**)(**Zëri**), **një pjesë e mirë e këtyre fjalëve kanë kaluar në historizma**: *a fair number of these words have become historic* (**Gramatika e gjuhës shqipe**.)

ii. Where a noun is used in the plural without any defining demonstrative or number, after a preposition governing the Ablative Case, the **-ve** form must be used.

6. There is no Vocative case as such. A few fossilised forms of a former Vocative can be found. These consist of the particle **O** (**oj** for feminine nouns), which can be placed before the noun or used as a suffix.

7. When addressing individuals by name the Indefinite Form of the Nominative is used.

8. There is no Locative case in modern Albanian. Where, however, a simple place-name is preceded by **në**, the Indefinite Form of the Accusative is used. To express location, either a preposition can be used, or the noun can be used in the Ablative case of the Definite Form, as in **malit**: *in the mountains*, **fushës**: *in the fields, on the plain*, **rrugës**: *along the road*. In the plural this meaning is conveyed by the Indefinite Form of the Ablative, as in **malesh**: *in the mountains*.

V   **DEFINITENESS**

1. The difference between the Definite and Indefinite Forms of the Albanian Noun is comparable to the difference marked in English by the use of the Definite Article *the* and the Indefinite Article *a/an* respectively. In Albanian the Indefinite Forms are frequently preceded by an "Indefinite definer": **një**: *a, one* in the Singular and **ca**: *some* or **disa**: *some* in the Plural, and under certain circumstances must be preceded by one of these: see Paragraph 15 below. A full treatment of the usage of the Definite and Indefinite Forms is outside the scope of this work.

2. The Definite Form may be used only where a noun is a syntactical part of a clause or sentence, i.e. as subject

or object, or when governed by a preposition or a Clitic.

3. Sometimes the use of the Definite or Indefinite is determined by a preceding preposition. **Nga, kah** and **te** are followed by the Definite Form of the Nominative case unless the noun is qualified by a an Indefinite definer or a cardinal number, as in:

I shoqeruar ...nga tri anëtarë të këshillit: *accompanied by three members of the council* (Zija Çela, **Lëngata e hënës.**)

4. Cardinal numbers and demonstratives such as **ky/kjo** and **ai/ajo** are normally followed by Indefinite Forms. However where a number refers to a specified group, the noun will be in the Definite Form and the number will take a feminine ending if qualifying a feminine noun, e.g.

të katër djemtë: *the four boys,* **të dyja motrat**: *the two* (or *both*) *sisters*.

5. The overriding ("Single Definite Element") principle is that only one word in a phrase can be in the Definite Form, unless separated by a Clitic following a Genitive case. However a surname will remain in the Definite Form when preceded by a title, as in:

Kryetari Ibrahim Rugova.

6. The most obvious illustration of the "Single Definite Element" principle is found in personal names, where the first name will, when followed by a surname, appear in the Indefinite Form. There is an increasing tendency for feminine names ending in **-ë** to be

replaced by the Definite Form ending in **-a**, as in **Flora Brovina, Violeta Qirici**.

7. Proper names are used in the Definite Form except:

a. Where a first name is followed by a surname:

   Naim Frashëri, Ramiz Kelmendi.

b. Where a name is in apposition:

   Në qytetin Tetovë, në fshatin Crep, Mbreti Zog.

c. When used predicatively:

   Babai e quan Petrit: *(his) father calls him Petrit*.

d. When used as a form of address:

   Mirëmëngjesi Kosovë! Mirë se ardhur, Fatmir.

   Rafete, si jeni? Shpresë, a ke kryer?

e. Following a preposed adjective:

   I dituri Hetem: *the learned Hetem*.

f. Following the prepositions **në** and **prej**:

   Në Zhegër: *in Zhegra*, **prej Durrësi**: *from Durrës*.

g. When specifying the origin of an animal or product:

   Verë Rahoveci: *wine from Rahovec*.

8. Demonstratives such as **ky** and **ai** define the noun so that the following noun will take the Indefinite Form.

9. In the idiomatic construction where the adjective precedes the noun the adjective will take the Definite Form, the noun the Indefinite.

10. Cardinal Numbers such as **shtatë**: *seven*, **nëntëmbëdhjetë**: *nineteen* will generally be followed by the Indefinite Form, unless the speaker is referring to a number of known beings or objects, in which case the Clitic **të** is used, as in:

   të gjashtë vëllimet: *the six volumes.*

   When referring to a numbered group referred to previously, the clitic may be omitted, as in:

   Gjenerali, prifti dhe tre shqiptarët u ulën (Ismail Kadare, **Gjenerali i ushtrisë së vdekur**.)

11. Cardinal numbers used with the clitic **të** and the Definite Form may also imply completeness, as in:

   të tridhjetë kommunat e Kosovës: *the* (or *all*) *thirty municipalities of Kosova*, and **në të dy** (or **dyja**) **rastet**: *on both occasions.*

12. Ordinal numbers, on the other hand, will follow nouns in the Definite Form.

13. The Definite Form is used when a noun of any type is used generically, as in:

   Rrugat asfaltohen kur afrohen zgjedhet: *roads are resurfaced when elections approach* (**Koha ditore**).

14. The Definite Form is used where a noun is followed by a second noun in the Genitive case; the second noun will also take the Definite Form, as for example:

Drejtori i shkollës: *the principal of the school.*

However either or both nouns in a phrase of this type can be made Indefinite if the context requires by the use of a modifier, viz. **një**: *a, one* in the Singular and **ca**: *some* or **disa**: *some* in the Plural.

15. The Genitive, Dative and Ablative cases of the Indefinite Form may not be used unless the noun is preceded by a demonstrative (**këtij/kësaj, atij/asaj**) or an indefinite defining expression such as **disa**, **ca**, or **ndonje**, or is used descriptively, as in **Verë Rahoveci**.

16. The Definite Form is formed as follows (in outline):

a. Masculine and feminine nouns ending in -**ë** drop this letter before the Definite Form ending, while nouns with -**ë** in the final syllable (i.e. almost all nouns of both genders ending in -**ël**, -**ër** and -**ërr**) drop the **ë**.

b. The Definite Form of the Nominative singular of First Declension masculine nouns is normally formed by adding -**i** to the CF. For Second Declension nouns the ending is -**u**. In both Declensions the Nominative Singular Definite is identical to the Oblique cases of the Indefinite Form.

c. Some First Declension nouns extend or alter the stem:

Group Feature	Addition/ alteration	Specimen CF	Nom. Def. /Obl. Indef
5. Stressed vowel ending	Adds -**ri** to CF Adds -**ni** to CF	**zë** **dry**	**zëri** **dryni**
6. Stem in -**ua** or -**uall** (not **huall** and **truall**)	-**ua** to -**oi** -**uall** to -**olli**	**thua** **fashuall**	**thoi** **fasholli**

45

d. Feminine nouns form the Nominative Singular Definite by replacing final -**ë** or unstressed -**e** with -**a** or -**ja**, or adding one of these to the stem.

e. The Nominative singular Definite Form of neuter nouns is formed by adding -**t**, -**ët** or -**të** to the CF.

17. A few nouns form the Definite Form irregularly:

a. From the First Declension:

Pëlqyer: *thumb* and **gavyell**: *rim* (of cartwheel) shed the **y** of the stem: Definite Forms are **pëlqeri** and **gavelli**.

b. From the Second Declension:

i. **Krye**: *head* when used as a masculine noun becomes **kreu** in the Definite Form, also retaining this stem in the Oblique cases of the Indefinite Form, and throughout the plural.

ii. **Bej**: *bej, landowner* sheds the final **j** in all singular declined forms, declining regularly, with the stem **be-**, as does the name **Skënderbej**.

18. For surnames ending in -**aj** and -**ej** the Definite and Indefinite Nominative Singular Forms are identical: the Definite Forms take suffixes -**n** and -**t** in the other cases; sometimes the suffixes -**un** and -**ut** are seen.

19. Place names ending in -**aj**, -**ej** and -**oj** with the stress on or before the penultimate syllable decline as above, but those few with the stress on the last syllable, such as **Bilanáj** and **Synéj**, also monosyllabics such as **Xhaj**, add the normal suffixes in the Definite Form.

20. Foreign names of either gender which end in an **-i** with stress on or before the penultimate syllable do not have a separate Definite Form, and belong to the First Declension regardless of gender. Examples include:

Xhoni: *Johnnie*, **Meri**: *Mary* and **derbi**: *game or match between two local teams* (local Derby).

VI CITATION

1. The Nominative Singular Indefinite Form of the noun is the normal Citation Form. Where the noun exists only in the plural, the Citation Form will be the Nominative Plural Indefinite.

2. The Citation Form is used for grammatical and lexicographic purposes.

3. Articulated nouns are listed under the noun itself, with the Clitic in brackets afterwards.

4. Although Proper Nouns are generally used in the Definite Form, their Citation Form is (except as below) the Indefinite Form.

5. This convention generally applies to place-names as shown on maps, although some recent maps show Definite Forms; however, where a Common Noun is used to designate a location, area or geographical feature, it will appear in the Definite Form, as for example:

Qafa, Kodra e Trimave, Gryka e Kaçanikut, Përroi i Desivojcës.

6. A place name which is qualified, such as **Gadime e Poshtme** may be shown in either form.

7. In English publications it is conventional for place names ending in **ë** to be rendered in the Definite Form, e.g. **TIRANA**.

VII NEUTER NOUNS

1. There are four categories of neuter nouns, namely gerunds, articulated nouns which are substantivised adjectives, a few substance nouns and the nouns **ballë** and **krye**. However the neuter gender is moribund in present-day Albanian, and the tendency therefore is to treat such nouns, with exceptions, as masculine or feminine, as explained below. They do not normally have plural forms, except as detailed below, and such plurals as there are become feminine in gender, adding the suffix **-a**, except for **krye**, which uses the plural of its masculine form, namely **krerë**.

2. Gerunds and articulated nouns derived from adjectives can immediately be distinguished by the preceding Clitic **të** or, in one usage, **së**.

3. Gerunds are identical in form (in the Citation Form) to the Participle of the verb from which they are derived, and invariably (except in the instance below) preceded by the Clitic **të**. When used in the plural they become grammatically feminine. The Ablative of the Gerund is also used with **me së** to express *with* or *from ...ing*, as: **INA e Zagrebit nuk ka pushuar me së kërkuari të drejtën e pronësisë**: *INA of Zagreb has not ceased pressing for its rights of ownership* (**Koha ditore**).

4. Increasingly Gerunds are being replaced by Deverbal Nouns ending in **-im** and **-je**. Also increasingly the feminine clitic is used before a participle to form a gerundial noun, replacing the neuter form.

5. Neuter nouns which are substantivised adjectives, such as **të ftohtë**: *cold*, **të verdhë**: *jaundice* (literally: *yellow*) usually refer to basic concepts such as heat (or cold), light (or darkness) and colour (often describing an illness or its most obvious symptom), and are used only in the singular.

6. There is also a small number of nouns mostly denoting substances; those of them which form a plural do so with the suffix **-ra**, and become feminine in the plural. Their meaning is subtly altered, thus:

gjashtë djathëra means *six types of cheese*.

7. They generally decline as masculine nouns of the First Declension, and the neuter forms are nowadays used only for stylistic effect or in certain set expressions. The most common nouns of this type are as follows:

a. Ending in **-ë**:

Indefinite	Meaning	Definite
brumë	*dough*	**brumët**
djathë	*cheese*	**djathët**
drithë	*grain*	**drithët**
dyllë	*wax*	**dyllët**
dhallë	*buttermilk*	**dhallët**
dhjamë	*tallow*	**dhjamët**
grurë	*stone*	**grurët**
gjalpë	*butter*	**gjalpët**
mjaltë	*honey*	**mjaltët**
ujë	*water*	**ujët**

b. Ending in a consonant:

lesh	*hair*	**leshtë**
miell	*honey*	**mielltë**
mish	*meat*	**mishtë**
vaj	*oil*	**vajtë**

8. **Ballë**: *forehead* and **krye**: *head* (as a part of the body) are still used as neuter nouns, forming the Definite Form with the ending -**t**, as in **ballët** and **kryet**. **Ballë** is, however, more often used as a masculine noun.

9. **Krye** has vestigial neuter forms: the Nominative Singular Definite is **kryet**. The plural of **krye** is **krerë**, which, as in English, can be used to number livestock: **krerë bagëtish**: *head of cattle*. When used to refer to a human, as in the person at the head of an organisation, or to the chapter of a book, it is masculine in both singular and plural forms, and follows the pattern of the Second Declension, with the Definite Form **kreu.** The neuter declension (Fourth Declension) is set out in Section XII.

VIII DECLENSION AND CASE FORMATION

1. Albanian nouns have five cases, and the various cases are distinguished by endings. Some endings, however, are shared by two or more cases. The pattern of shared endings differs between Definite and Indefinite Forms, and between singular and plural forms. These notes do not apply to neuter nouns, which are covered separately.

2. In the Indefinite Singular form the Nominative and Accusative forms are identical. The Oblique cases

(Genitive, Dative and Ablative) have an identical ending, which varies according to the declension of that noun. The Genitive case is preceded by a Clitic which varies according to the gender, number, case and form (Definite or Indefinite) of the preceding noun. Subject to a very few exceptions, the Oblique case ending for First Declension nouns is **-i**, or in a few nouns **-ri** or **-ni**: for Second Declension Nouns **-u**: for Third Declension Nouns **-e** or **-je**. For Fourth Declension nouns see the Declension Tables.

3. The plural is normally formed by the addition of a suffix: the most common are: **-ë**, **-a**, **-e**, **-ër**, **-ra** and **-nj**. Some nouns have identical singular and plural forms; others change a vowel or consonant in the stem, sometimes also adding endings. This is dealt with in detail in Sections XV and XVII.

4. Nouns with an Indefinite Nominative form ending in **-ël**, **-ëll**, **-ër**, **-ërr**, **-ul**, **-ull** and **-ur** may be masculine or feminine. Their gender can be established only from the ending of the Definite Form, or from the form of an adjective relating to that noun. The **ë** of the Indefinite Nominative/Accusative form disappears in all other cases of both Definite and Indefinite Forms, except in a very few instances. See Part F for details.

5. In the Definite Singular form of masculine nouns the Nominative case has a vowel ending (**-i**, **-ri** or **-ni** for nouns of the First Declension, or **-u** for Second Declension Nouns). The Accusative case adds **-n** to the Nominative (Definite) form, and the Oblique cases add **-t**. As with the Indefinite Form, the Genitive is preceded by a Clitic which varies according to the gender, number, case and form (Definite or Indefinite) of the preceding noun.

6. In the Definite Singular form of feminine nouns the Nominative case has a vowel ending (**-a** or **-ja/-ia**). The rules for the formation of the Oblique cases vary between the various groups. As with the Indefinite Form, the Genitive is preceded by a Clitic which varies according to the gender, number, case and form (Definite or Indefinite) of the preceding noun.

7 Masculine and feminine nouns form the Definite plural in an identical manner. The Nominative and Accusative forms are identical, and are normally formed as follows, by reference to the plural stem:

a. Nouns with stems ending in an unstressed vowel add **-t** to form the Nominative/Accusative forms, **-ve** for the Oblique cases, and **-sh** for the Indefinite Ablative.

b. Nouns with stems ending in two consonants or in **-l, -r, -s** or **-z** add **-it** to form the Nominative/Accusative forms, **-ve** for the Oblique cases, and **-ish** for the Indefinite Ablative.

c. Nouns with stems ending in a consonant other than **-l, -r, -s, -t or -z**, or in a stressed vowel, add **-të** to form the Nominative/Accusative forms, **-ve** for the Oblique cases, and **-sh** for the Indefinite Ablative. Nouns with plural stems ending in **-sh** form Ablative with **-ësh.**

d. Further details, and details of other small noun groups and of substantivised adjectives are at Section XIII (masculine nouns) and Section XVI (feminine nouns).

8. The declension of the plural forms depends on the ending of the plural stem rather than the Declension to which an individual noun belongs in the singular forms. For that reason it is dealt with separately from the Declensions of the singular forms. Where,

however, nouns of a Class are listed in the individual classes of the Singular Declension, and that Class can easily be sub-divided to show different plural endings, such subdivision has been made.

9. Compound nouns, with few exceptions, take the declension of their second (or final) element, thus **sivëlla**: *colleague* declines like **vëlla**: *brother*, and **rrokaqiell**: *skyscraper* like **qiell**: *sky*. For those with divergent plurals see Section XXI 7.

10. Exceptions, in which the first part declines and the second part remains unaltered, include:

a. All compound units of measurement such as **ditë-njeri**: *the work one man can do in a day* and **kalë-fuqi**: *horsepower*.

b. Most compounds of **peshk**: *fish* (not **peshkaqen**).

c. **Shtëpi-muze**: *house dedicated as museum* and **qytet-muze**: *preserved town*.

11. Compound nouns where the second element is an adjective do not always follow the exact plural or feminine form of the adjective. They should be checked individually in an authoritative dictionary.

12. **Togfjalësh**: *group of words* cannot decline its second part, because **fjalësh** is already in the Ablative, and cannot decline like **tog**, because it cannot belong to the Second Declension. Its ending therefore puts it in the First Declension and it forms plural with **-a**.

13. **Aeroplan**: *aeroplane* and **hidroplan**: *hydroplane* both form their plurals regularly with **-ë**, but **biplan**: *biplane* forms plural **biplane**.

IX   **THE FIRST DECLENSION**

1. General

a. Throughout this section all references to cases relate only to the singular cases, except where the plural is specifically mentioned.

b. This Declension includes all masculine nouns **except**:

i. Those which belong to the Second Declension, viz.

aa. Those ending in -**g**, -**h** and -**k**.

bb. Monosyllabics with vowel-endings, except those such as **zë** and **dry** which extend the stem with -**r** or -**n**.

cc. Most Nouns ending in a stressed vowel.

ii. Those nouns which denote male beings but end in -**e**, -**ë** or -**o** and form part of the Third Declension.

2. This Declension includes the following categories of nouns with vowel endings:

a. Nouns of two or more syllables ending with stressed -**a**, such as **baba**: *father*, **vëlla**: *brother* and **xhaxha**: *uncle* (*on father's side*). Also **hero**: *hero* and **afendiko:** *person who gives himself airs and graces* and certain foreign names (Group 4).

b. Nouns with stem extensions such as **zë** and **dry**.

c. Nouns ending in -**ua** (except **grua** and **hua**) (Gp. 6).

d. Nouns of foreign origin ending in unstressed -**i** (Gp.1).

3. Group 1

a. This group consists of nouns ending in a consonant (other than **-g**, **-h** or **-k**) and not falling into any other group, including those proper nouns (as listed in Part F) such as **Antigon** denoting females and ending in a consonant. Declension is:

	Indefinite	Definite
Nominative	**qytet**	**qyteti**
Accusative	**qytet**	**qytetin**
Genitive	**i/e qyteti**	**i/e qytetit**
Dative	**qyteti**	**qytetit**
Ablative	**qyteti**	**qytetit**

b. This group also includes foreign names ending in unstressed **-i**: first names such as **Meri**, surnames such as **Verdi**, geographical names such as **Havái**, and **derbi**: *local Derby* (sport), **sherri**: *sherry*, with identical Nominative Definite and Indefinite Forms.

	Indefinite	Definite
Nominative	**Meri**	**Meri**
Accusative		**Merin**
Genitive		**i/e Merit**
Dative/Ablative		**Merit**

c. **Fashuall** and **gërruall**, which change the stem to **-oll** to form the Oblique cases and the Definite Form, are listed under Group 6. **Huall** and **truall** do not alter the stem in the singular and so belong in Group 1.

d. **Gavyell**: *rim* (of cartwheel) and **pelqyer**: *thumb* change the stem to **gavell-** and **pelqer-** in all singular forms except the CF and Indefinite Accusative, and therefore belong to Group 6. The other nouns ending in **-yell** retain the **y** throughout the singular.

e. **Bej**: *bey* (Ottoman noble) belongs to the Second Declension.

4. Group 2

a. This group consists of (masculine) nouns ending in **-ël, -ëm, -ër** and **-ërr** which drop the **ë** in the Oblique cases of the Indefinite Form and throughout the Definite Form. Most of these nouns form the plural with **-a**, but for details of plurals and a list of the more common nouns with these endings see Part F.

b. Declension is as set out:

	Indefinite	Definite
Nominative	**emër**	**emri**
Accusative	**emër**	**emrin**
Genitive	**i/e emri**	**i/e emrit**
Dative/Abl.	**emri**	**emrit**

c. Nouns ending in **-ëll** retain the **ë** throughout, and therefore decline as Group 1 nouns.

d. Of the masculine nouns ending in **-ëm, prizëm, ritëm** and nouns of foreign origin ending in **-izëm** belong to this group. A few words as listed in Part F retain the **ë** of the stem throughout. For plurals see Part F.

e. The feminine noun **parzëm**: *breast* belongs to this Group.

f. **Hatër**: *favour*, **satër**: *meat-cleaver* and **talër**: *open vat* retain the **ë** throughout and form Plural with **-e**.

g. For the plurals of **drapër**: *sickle*, **gjarpër**: *snake* and **shpargër**: *nappy* see Section XV Class 13 and for **dhëndër**: *son-in-law* see Section XV Paragraph 18.

h. **Kërr**: *gray* (horse) and **cërr**: *wren* being monosyllabic retain the **ë** throughout their declension.

i. **Ipeshkëv**: *Roman Catholic bishop* (plural **ipeshkvij**) belongs to this group, as do **qehën**: *baker's shovel* (plural **qehna**) and **zgjebëç**: *clematis* (plural **zgjebça**).

j. The few masculine nouns ending in -**ëz** listed at Part F retain **ë** throughout and therefore belong in Group 1.

5. Group 3

a. This group consists of nouns ending in -**ë** as listed at II 6 iv *aa*. and *bb*. Plurals are listed under Class 11:

	Indefinite	Definite
Nominative	**burrë**	**burri**
Accusative	**burrë**	**burrin**
Genitive	**i/e burri**	**i/e burrit**
Dative/Ablative	**burri**	**burrit**

b. **Atë**: *father* is irregular: in the singular the stem vowel changes, and the singular Definite Form has two declensions, one of which is used after the Clitic representing the Third Person Singular Possessive. The declension is set out at XX 2.

i. In the singular **atë** is almost invariably used with a preposed possessive adjective, such as **im**. First and second person possessives are followed by the Indefinite Form, while third person possessives are followed by a variant of the Definite Form. There is a further Definite Form for use without a preposed possessive adjective. The plural forms are based on the **et** stem.

ii. **Atë** may also be spelt **at**, but should not be confused with **at**: *saddle horse*, which has plural form **atllarë**.

c. This group includes the substance nouns ending in **-ë** listed at Section VII together with **ballë**, all of which still have vestigial neuter forms. Those substance nouns which have a plural form this with **-(ë)ra**.

6. Group 4.

a. This group comprises a small number of animate nouns, all having two or more syllables, with stems ending in a stressed **-a** or **-o**. Monosyllabic masculine nouns ending in **-a** and other masculine nouns ending in a vowel belong to the Second Declension, apart from those specifically listed or categorised in the various groups of the First Declension.

b. These nouns decline as follows:

	Indefinite	Definite
Nominative	**vëlla**	**vëllai**
Accusative	**vëlla**	**vëllanë**
Genitive	**i/e vëllai**	**i/e vëllait**
Dative/Abl.	**vëllai**	**vëllait**

c. Also in this group are:

aga: *landowner* (Ottoman), **baba**: *father*, **budalla**: *fool*, **fukara**: *pauper*, **pasha**: *governor* (under Ottoman Empire), **xhaxha**, *uncle*, **hero**: *hero*, **afendiko**: *a person who gives himself airs and graces*, the archaic word **qehaja**: *bailiff*, also proper names stressed on the final **a** such as **Isá**, **Hamzá** and **Musá**.

d. Most nouns in this group form the plural with **-llarë**: the following are exceptions:

Singular	Meaning	Plural
budalla	*fool*	**budallenj**
fukara	*pauper*	**fukarenj**
maskara	*scoundrel*	**maskarenj**
qerrata	see dictionary	**qerratenj**
vëlla	*brother*	**vëllezër**
afendiko	*see above*	**afendikonj**
hero	*hero*	**heronj**

e. Apart from **hero** and **afendiko** the only other nouns ending in -o which belong to this group are surnames of foreign (usually French) origin, such as:

Xha Gorioi: *Père Goriot* (novel by Balzac) and **Nipi i Ramoit**: *le neveu de Rameau*, by **Didero**: *Diderot*.

f. Other nouns ending in -o are Third Declension nouns.

g. **Kalama**: *child, immature person* extends the stem with -n and therefore belongs to Group 5.

h. Of the inanimate nouns ending in a stressed -a, **vulla**: *strip of land* and **rogja**: *arm of delta* extend the stem with -n and therefore belong to Group 5, while **syka**: *garden anemone* belongs to the Second Declension.

i. **Jenisé**: *Yenisej* and **Pompé**: *Pompeii* have Definite Forms in -i. These are the original Russian and Latin names, the Indefinite being a back-formation.

7. Group 5

a. This group consists of nouns ending in a stressed vowel and monosyllabics which extend the stem by adding -r in the Oblique cases of the Indefinite Form and throughout the Definite Form. A few nouns extend the stem with -n. For plurals see Class 12.

b. They decline as follows:

	Indefinite	Definite
Nominative	zë	zëri
Accusative	zë	zërin
Genitive	i/e zëri	i/e zërit
Dative/Ablative	zëri	zërit

c. The normal pattern of declension is for the stem to be extended with -r as shown above but for the extension to disappear in the plural, which is formed with -nj, as **pe/peri/penj**, **mulli/mulliri/mullinj**. Nouns which follow this pattern are listed at XV 12 b i.

d. Some nouns retain the -r stem extension in the plural, forming the plural with -rë as shown below. Nouns which follow this pattern are listed at XV 12 c.

Indefinite	Meaning	Definite	Plural
tra	*beam*	**trari**	**trarë**

e. **Drunj** is the plural of the Feminine noun **dru**: *firewood*.

f. **Tra** has both First and Second Declension forms: of its compounds **kryetra**: *architrave, lintel* has only First Declension forms, while **arkitra**: *architrave* has only Second Declension forms.

g. **Qiri**: *candle* also has Second Declension forms.

h. **Li**: *flax* (Definite **liri**) and **gjë**: *livestock* (Definite **gjëri**) have no plural forms listed in **Fjalor. sh. s.**

i. The following form the plural differently:

Indefinite	Meaning	Definite	Plural
shullë	sunny place	shullëri	shullëre
zë	voice	zëri	zëra
hi	cinders	hiri	hira
kufi	border	kufiri	kufij
tru	brain	truri	tru
gju	knee	gjuri	gjunjë
sy	eye	syri	sy

j. The following extend the stem with -**ni** instead of -**ri**.

i. Forming plural in -**nj**:

Indefinite	Meaning	Definite	Plural
kacara	cudgel	kacarani	kacaranj
vulla	strip of land	vullani	vullanj
arne	Heldreich pine	arneni	arnenj
bli	sturgeon	blini	blinj
buli	water elm	bulini	bulinj
ulpëti	wych elm	ulpëtini	ulpëtinj
galacu	paralytic	galacuni	galacunj
kacabu	cockroach	kacabuni	kacabunj

ii. Forming plural in -**j**:

Indefinite	Meaning	Definite	Plural
kalama	child*	kalamani	kalamaj
rogja	branch of delta	rogjani	rogjaj
mëti	churn	mëtini	mëtij

iii. Other plurals:

Indefinite	Meaning	Definite	Plural
hu	see dictionary	huni	hu
dry	padlock	dryni	dryna

k. **Mëllë** is stressed on the last syllable, as is its plural.

l. **Bli/bliri/blirë**: *lime tree* and **hu/huri/hunj**: *pole, stake* have homonyms viz. **bli/blini/blinj**: *sturgeon* and **hu/huni/hu**: *crowd* or *hundredweight*.

8. Group 6.

a. This group consists primarily of nouns ending in **-ua** which in the singular alter the stem to **-o** in the Oblique cases of the Indefinite Form and throughout the Definite Form, and almost all form the plural with **-onj**. Irregular formations are also listed in Class 13. The group also includes **fashuall**: *honeycomb*, **gërruall**: *tub formed from tree stump*, **gavyell**: *rim* (of cartwheel) and **pëlqyer**: *thumb*.

b. Declension is as follows:

	Indefinite	Definite
Nominative	**thua**	**thoi**
Accusative	**thua**	**thoin/ thuan**
Genitive	**i/e thoi**	**i/e thoit**
Dative/Abl.	**thoi**	**thoit**

c. **Grua** and **hua** are feminine and decline accordingly (See Section XI, Third Declension, Group 6).

d. **Fashuall**: *honeycomb* and **gërruall**: *wooden tub fashioned from tree stump* decline similarly to the above, altering the stem to **fasholl-** and **gërroll-**. The Oblique Indefinite and Nominative Definite Forms are therefore **fasholli** and **gërrolli** respectively.

e. **Gavyell**: *rim* (of cartwheel) and **pëlqyer**: *thumb* form Definite **gavelli** and **pëlqeri** respectively and plurals **gavej** and **pëlqerë**, i.e. the **y** appears only in the CF and Indefinite Accusative. Other nouns ending in

-**yell** retain the **y** in the singular forms and therefore belong to Group 1. They drop the **y** in plural forms.

9. Groups 7 & 8 have no counterpart in this Declension.

10. Group 9: Substantivised adjectives:

a. The Clitic preceding a substantivised adjective does not follow the same pattern as the normal Adjectival/Genitive Clitic: also the Clitic for all plural forms is **të**.

b. Examples are:

i. Consonant stem (as per Group 1):

	Indefinite	Definite
Nominative	**i ditur**	**i dituri**
Accusative	**të ditur**	**të diturin**
Genitive	**i/e të dituri**	**i/e të diturit**
Dative/Abl.	**të dituri**	**të diturit**

ii Disappearing **ë** in final syllable (as per Group 2):

	Indefinite	Definite
Nominative	**i vogël**	**i vogli**
Accusative	**të vogël**	**të voglin**
Genitive	**i/e të vogli**	**i/e të voglit**
Dative/Abl.	**të vogli**	**të voglit**

iii. Stem ending in -**ë** (as per Group 3):

	Indefinite	Definite
Nominative	**i aftë**	**i afti**
Accusative	**të aftë**	**të aftin**
Genitive	**i/e të afti**	**i/e të aftit**
Dative/Abl.	**të afti**	**të aftit**

X   THE SECOND DECLENSION

1. This Declension comprises those masculine nouns which do not belong to the First and Third Declensions, specifically:

a. Nouns ending in **-g**, **-h** and **-k**.

b. Monosyllabic nouns with vowel-endings (except those in Group 5 of the First Declension and those in the Third Declension).

c. Nouns ending in a stressed vowel, notably those nouns of Turkish origin (many obsolete, and some derogatory) ending in **-çi** and **-xhi**, such as **sahatçi**: *watchmaker* and **kalemxhi**: *scribbler, hack writer*, and some in **-li** such as **borxhli**: *debtor*.

d. **Bej**: *bej* (see 4 c opposite) and **krye**: *head*.

2. Declension is similar to that of the First Declension, except that **-u** replaces **-i** as the stem extension. The numbering of the Declension Groups is aligned to that of the First Declension

3. Group 1: Ending in consonant (**-g**, **-h** and **-k**):

a. Declension is as follows:

	Indefinite	Definite
Nominative	shok	shoku
Accusative	shok	shokun
Genitive	i/e shoku	i/e shokut
Dat/Abl	shoku	shokut

b. Nouns of this group mostly form the plural with **-ë**.

4. Group 4: Ending in a vowel:

a. Declension is as follows:

	Indefinite	Definite
Nominative	**dhe**	**dheu**
Accusative	**dhe**	**dheun**
Genitive	**i/e dheu**	**i/e dheut**
Dat/Abl	**dheu**	**dheut**

b. The set phrase **fjala mori dhenë**: *the news spread* preserves an archaic and obsolete declension form.

c. **Bej**: *bey* (Ottoman title) belongs to this Declension. The stem reduces to **be-** in the singular, and the plural is **bejlerë**. The name **Skënderbej** declines likewise.

d. Second Declension nouns ending in a vowel by definition belong to Class 12. Exceptions are:

i. Class 1

mulla	*mullah*	**trofe**	*trophy*
va	*ford*	**turne**	*tournament*
jubile	*jubilee*	**gjeni**	*genius* (person)
lice	*lyceum*	**mazi**	*oak-gall*
muze	*museum*	**thi**	*boar*

ii. Irregular

arkitra	*architrave*	**arkitrarë**
ka	*ox*	**qe**
tra	*beam*	**trarë**
ble	*volume* (of book)	**blej**
derebe	*Feudal official* (Ottoman)	**derebej**
dhe	*earth**	**dhera**
she	*perennial stream*	**shera**

haxhi	*hajji*	**haxhilerë**
njeri	*man, person*	**njerëz**
shi	*rain*	**shira**

e. For **syká**: *garden anemone* or *oxeye*, **apogje**: *apogee*, **perigje**: *perigee* and **dra**: *dregs, lees* **Fjalor sh. s.** does not list a plural. **Egje**: *Aegean Sea* and **Mesdhe**: *Mediterranean Sea* have no plural.

f. **Qiri**: *candle* and **tra**: *beam* have both First (**zë** Class) and Second Declension forms: **arkitra**: *architrave* has only Second Declension forms.

g. In Gheg usage **tra** with the meaning *attic, loft* always takes Second Declension endings and has plural **tra**.

h. The geographical names **Tuválu** and **Bissáu** do not have separate Indefinite Forms (cf. **Havái**).

i. **Jeremi**: *hermit* belongs to this group but also has Third Declension forms. It remains masculine.

5. Group 7. (**krye** only):

	Indefinite	Definite
Nominative	**krye**	**kreu**
Accusative	**krye**	**kreun**
Genitive	**i/e kreu**	**i/e kreut**
Dative/ Abl.	**kreu**	**kreut**

6. Group 9: Substantivised adjective:

	Indefinite	Definite
Nominative	**i ri**	**i riu**
Accusative	**të ri**	**të riun**
Genitive	**i/e të riu**	**i/e të riut**
Dative/Abl.	**të riu**	**të riut**

XI THE THIRD DECLENSION

1. This declension consists of all feminine nouns, except for a very small number as listed in Part F Section III, together with a small number of masculine nouns, the most common of which are listed at Part F, Section IV. The Declension Groups have been numbered to correspond with those of the masculine Declensions, at the price of placing minor groups before major.

2. Group 1: nouns ending in **-uar**, **-ul**, **-ull** and **-ur**:

	Indefinite	Definite
Nominative	**kumbull**	**kumbulla**
Accusative	**kumbull**	**kumbullën**
Genitive	**i/e kumbulle**	**i/e kumbullës**
Dative/Abl.	**kumbulle**	**kumbullës**

3. Group 2

This group contains nouns ending in **-ël**, **-ër** or **-ërr**. In those cases which take an ending, i.e. all cases apart from the Nominative and Accusative (Singular) Indefinite, the -ë disappears:

	Indefinite	Definite
Nominative	**motër**	**motra**
Accusative	**motër**	**motrën**
Genitive	**i/e motre**	**i/e motrës**
Dative/Abl.	**motre**	**motrës**

4. Group 3

a. This group consists of nouns ending in -ë, which in the Oblique Indefinite cases drop the -ë and add -e. In the Definite Form the Nominative ends in **-a**, the

67

Accusative in **-ën** and the Oblique cases in **-ës**. The overwhelming majority of feminine nouns belongs to this Group: **gjë**: *thing* (monosyllabic) is in Group 5.

b. Declension:

	Indefinite	Definite
Nominative	**ditë**	**dita**
Accusative	**ditë**	**ditën**
Genitive	**i/e dite**	**i/e ditës**
Dative/Abl.	**dite**	**ditës**

c. Most nouns with this ending, and in particular animate nouns, form the plural with **-a**. However a significant number has a plural form identical to the CF.

d. This group includes **fëmijë**: *child*, which is masculine, and those nouns ending in **-ë** denoting male persons which belong to the Third Declension.

i. With plural identical to CF:

dukë	*duke*	**kallfë**	*apprentice*
fëmijë	*child*	**lalë**	*older person**
gegë	*Gheg*	**papë**	*Pope*
judë	*Judas, betrayer*	**toskë**	*Tosk*

ii. Forming plural with **-allarë**:

axhë	*uncle* (father's brother)
dajë	*uncle* (mother's brother)
hoxhë	*Holy man, muezzin*

iii. **Dajë** has alternative plural **daja**.

iv. **Bacë**: *uncle/ elder brother* forms plural **baca**, and the Gheg word **mixhë**: *uncle* (= **axha**) has plural **mixha**.

5. Group 4

a. This group consists of nouns ending in a stressed **-i**, which, except for **zotëri**, have identical singular and plural stems. It includes abstract nouns ending in **-ri** and **-si**.

b. Declension is as follows:

	Indefinite	Definite
Nominative	**shtëpi**	**shtëpia**
Accusative	**shtëpi**	**shtëpinë**
Genitive	**i/e shtëpie**	**i/e shtëpisë**
Dative/Abl.	**shtëpie**	**shtëpisë**

c. **Zotëri**: *lord* and **jeremi**: *hermit* belong to this Group but are grammatically masculine, and often declined as Second Declension nouns, forming plural with **-nj**.

6. Group 5

a. This group consists of nouns ending in stressed **-a, -e, -o, -u** and **-y**, and also acronyms and abbreviations. Declension resembles that of Group 4, except that **j** is inserted before the ending of the Nominative Singular Definite. The stress is on the final syllable of the stem throughout. Declension is:

	Indefinite	Definite
Nominative	**rrufe**	**rrufeja**
Accusative	**rrufe**	**rrufenë**
Genitive	**i/e rrufeje**	**i/e rrufesë**
Dative/Abl.	**rrufeje**	**rrufesë**

b. This group includes: **kala**: *castle*, **gjë**: *thing*, **byro**: *office*, **tablo**: *tableau*, **atu**: *trump card*, **dru**: *firewood*, **menu**: *menu*, **pardesy**: *trench coat* and **revy**: *revue*.

c. The singular and plural stems of nouns in this Group are identical, except for the following:

dru	*firewood*	**dru/drunj**
gjë	*thing*	**gjëra**
pëlle	*milch cow* (or other milking animal)	**pëlla**
rixha	*request* (archaic)	**rixhara**

d. Surnames of foreign origin ending in stressed -o decline as First Declension nouns.

7. Group 6

a. This group consists of the two feminine nouns ending in -**ua**, **grua**: *woman* and **hua**: *loan*. While the stress in **grua** falls on the **u**, **hua** is stressed on the **a**.

b. Declension is as follows:

	Indefinite	Definite
Nominative	**grua**	**gruaja**
Accusative	**grua**	**gruan**
Genitive	**i/e gruaje**	**i/e gruas**
Dative/Abl.	**gruaje**	**gruas**

c. **Grua** forms plural **gra**: **hua** belongs to Class 1F.

8. Group 7

a. This group consists of nouns ending in unstressed -**e**, which add -**je** to form the Oblique cases of the Indefinite Form, and those feminine nouns ending in unstressed -**o**, such as **radio**. In the Definite Form the final -**e** disappears in the Nominative, but is present in the other cases. The stress remains on the stem throughout, and they belong to FPG 2. Declension is:

	Indefinite	Definite
Nominative	**rreze**	**rrezja**
Accusative	**rreze**	**rrezen**
Genitive	**i/e rrezeje**	**i/e rrezes**
Dative/Abl.	**rrezeje**	**rrezes**

b. Nouns ending in **-ge** and **-ne** such as **bege**: *white grape*, **filologe**: *(female) philologist*, **banane**: *banana*, **kone**: *puppy*, **dibrane**: *woman from Dibër* and **fizikane**: *(female) physicist* decline as follows:

	Indefinite	Definite
Nominative	**banane**	**banania**
Accusative	**banane**	**bananen**
Genitive	**i/e bananeje**	**i/e bananes**
Dative/Abl.	**bananeje**	**bananes**

c. Nouns ending in **-gje** decline as follows:

	Indefinite	Definite
Nominative	**lagje**	**lagjja**
Accusative	**lagje**	**lagjen**
Genitive	**i/e lagjeje**	**i/e lagjes**
Dative/Abl.	**lagjeje**	**lagjes**

d. Nouns ending in unstressed **-o** decline as below:

	Indefinite	Definite
Nominative	**radio**	**radioja**
Accusative	**radio**	**radion**
Genitive	**i/e radioje**	**i/e radios**
Dative/Abl.	**radioje**	**radios**

e. The masculine noun **palaço**: *clown* also belongs to this group. Likewise **qole**: *servile person*, **qose**: *beardless person*, and **honxhoboxho**: *charlatan**.

f. A few masculine nouns describing people and animals by a physical feature or colouring belong to this group. They include **balo**: *dog or ox with white-spotted face* or *rogue* and **kuqo**: *person with reddish hair and florid complexion, red-coloured animal.*

g. Of the geographical names in this Group **San Marino**: (Republic of) *San Marino* is masculine.

h. **Bóa**: *boa constrictor* does not have separate Definite and Indefinite Forms in the Nominative singular.

9. Group 8.

Nouns with a CF ending in **-je** or **-ie** (after **-g-** and **-n-**), including the large group of deverbal nouns, decline as follows:

a. Nouns ending in **-je**:

	Indefinite	Definite
Nominative	**larje**	**larja**
Accusative	**larje**	**larjen**
Genitive	**i/e larjeje**	**i/e larjes**
Dative/Abl.	**larjeje**	**larjes**

Ndenjje: *sitting*, has Definite Form **ndenjja**.

b. Nouns ending in **-ie**:

	Indefinite	Definite
Nominative	**parathënie**	**parathënia**
Accusative	**parathënie**	**parathënien**
Genitive	**i/e parathënieje**	**i/e parathënies**
Dative/Abl.	**parathënieje**	**parathënies**

10. Group 9

a. This group consists of Substantivised Adjectives.

b. Stem ending in consonant, declining as per Group 1. In practice these are mostly participles ending in **-ur, -uar** and **-yer**, but with a few adjectives from ADG 2 (see Part B) such as **i shkathët** and **i dobët**:

	Indefinite	Definite
Nominative	**e mësuar**	**e mësuara**
Accusative	**të mësuar**	**të mësuarën**
Genitive	**i/e të mësuare**	**i/e të mësuarës**
Dat/ Abl	**të mësuare**	**të mësuarës**

c. Consonant stem shedding -**ë** from last syllable (as per Group 2):

	Indefinite	Definite
Nominative	**e ëmbël**	**e ëmbla**
Accusative	**të ëmbël**	**të ëmblën**
Genitive	**i/e të ëmble**	**i/e të ëmblës**
Dat/Abl	**të ëmble**	**të ëmblës**

d. Stem ending in -**ë** (as per Group 3):

	Indefinite	Definite
Nominative	**e drejtë**	**e drejta**
Accusative	**të drejtë**	**të drejtën**
Genitive	**i/e të drejte**	**i/e së drejtës**
Dat/Abl	**të drejte**	**së drejtës**

e. Stem ending in unstressed -**e**:

	Indefinite	Definite
Nominative	**e epërme**	**e epërmja**
Accusative	**të epërme**	**të epërmen**
Genitive	**i/e të epërmeje**	**i/e të epërmes**
Dat/ Abl.	**të epërmeje**	**të epërmes**

XII THE FOURTH DECLENSION

1. This declension consists of neuter nouns and has two principal groups, namely Gerunds and neuter nouns formed from adjectives. Again the Declension Groups have been aligned as far as possible, but there are no counterparts to Declension Groups 2, 5, 6 and 8. The Declension Groups have been subdivided into articulated and unarticulated nouns where appropriate. As to plurals, Groups 1a and 3a form plurals in **-a**, and Groups 1b and 3b form plurals in **-ëra**. All neuter nouns except **krye** become feminine in the plural.

2. Group 1a: Articulated nouns (Gerunds) formed from participles ending in **-ur** and **-uar**, and from adjectives ending in **-t**:

	Indefinite	Definite
Nom/Acc.	**të folur**	**të folurit**
Genitive	**i/e të foluri**	**i/e të folurit**
Dative/Abl.	**të foluri**	**të folurit**

Examples of adjectives forming neuter nouns in this group are **të errët**: *darkness*, **të mugët**: *twilight*.

3. Group 1b: Nouns (unarticulated) now rarely found as neuters ending in a consonant (more usually First Declension):

	Indefinite	Definite
Nom./Acc.	**mish**	**mishtë**
Genitive	**i/e mishi**	**i/e mishit**
Dative/Abl.	**mishi**	**mishit**

4. Group 3a: Articulated nouns ending in **-ë**, including gerunds formed from participles ending in **-në** and **-rë**:

	Indefinite	Definite
Nom./Acc.	**të ftohtë**	**të ftohtët**
Genitive	**i/e të ftohti**	**i/e të ftohtit**
Dative/Abl.	**të ftohti**	**të ftohtit**

5. Group 3b: Nouns (unarticulated) now rarely found as neuters ending in -ë (more usually First Declension):

	Indefinite	Definite
Nom.Acc.	**ujë**	**ujët**
Genitive	**i/e uji**	**i/e ujit**
Dative/Abl.	**uji**	**ujit**

6. Group 4: Nouns ending in vowel:

	Indefinite	Definite
Nom.Acc.	**të zi**	**të zitë**
Genitive	**i/e të ziu**	**i/e të zitë**
Dative/Abl.	**të ziu**	**të zitë**

7. Group 7: Noun ending in unstressed vowel: **krye**:

	Indefinite	Definite
Nominative	**krye**	**kryet**
Accusative	**krye**	**kryet**
Genitive	**i/e kreje**	**i/e kresë**
Dative/Abl.	**kreje**	**kresë**

8. Group 9: Other nouns formed from adjectives and ending in a consonant other than -t:

	Indefinite	Definite
Nom./Acc.	**të kuq**	**të kuqtë**
Genitive	**i/e të kuq**	**i/e të kuqtë**
Dative/Abl.	**të kuq**	**të kuqtë**

XIII PLURAL DECLENSION: MASCULINE NOUNS

Note: Throughout this Section and Section XIV references to the stem are to the Plural Indefinite stem.

1. MPG 1

   Nouns with stem ending in -ë:

	Indefinite	Definite
Nominative	studentë	studentët
Accusative	studentë	studentët
Genitive	i/e studentëve	i/e studentëve
Dative	studentëve	studentëve
Ablative	studentësh/ studentëve	studentëve

   As well as masculine (mostly animate) nouns forming the plural with -ë, this Group includes those Third Declension masculine nouns which belong to Class 1.

2. MPG 2

   Nouns with unstressed vowel ending, or ending in -uj, -uaj, -iej and -yej:

	Indefinite	Definite
Nominative	emra	emrat
Accusative	emra	emrat
Genitive	i/e emrave	i/e emrave
Dative	emrave	emrave
Ablative	emrash/ emrave	emrave

   This Group includes nouns forming the plural with -a, -e and -ra, polysyllabic nouns with singular stem ending in -ul and -ull, Class 3 nouns with singular stems ending in -uall, -iell and -yell, except those where the diphthong changes to a single vowel in the plural, also duaj (plural only): *sheaves*, **të huaj**: *foreigners*, **kuaj**, **muaj** and **lepuj**, and, from Class 12, **kalamaj** and **mëtij**.

3. MPG 3: Nouns with stem ending in a stressed vowel, or stressed vowel + **j**:

	Indefinite	Definite
Nominative	**qe**	**qetë**
Accusative	**qe**	**qetë**
Genitive	**i/e qeve**	**i/e qeve**
Dative	**qeve**	**qeve**
Ablative	**qesh/ qeve**	**qeve**

This group, which takes the same endings as MPG 5, consists of: **hyj** and **qe**, together with:

a. A few nouns with vowel stems from Class 1.

b. A few nouns from Class 12 which form the plural by adding **-j** to a stressed vowel ending.

4. MPG 4

Nouns with stem ending in **-l**, **-r**, **-s** and **-z**:

	Indefinite	Definite
Nominative	**mësues**	**mësuesit**
Accusative	**mësues**	**mësuesit**
Genitive	**i/e mësuesve**	**i/e mësuesve**
Dative	**mësuesve**	**mësuesve**
Ablative	**mësuesish/ mësuesve**	**mësuesve**

This Group consists mainly of Class 1 nouns ending in **-s**, and Class 14 nouns, which have plurals ending in **-ër**. **Gjelazez**: *cormorant* belongs to MPG 5.

5. MPG 5: Nouns with stem ending in a single consonant other than -j, -l, -r, -s, -t and -z, all of which are either monosyllabic or stressed on the final syllable:

	Indefinite	Definite
Nominative	miq	miqtë
Accusative	miq	miqtë
Genitive	i/e miqve	i/e miqve
Dative	miqve	miqve
Ablative	miqsh/ miqve	miqve

This group consists primarily of Class 3 nouns with plurals in vowel + **q** and vowel + **gj**, also nouns which form the plural with **-nj**, and the following (plural forms given): **kuleç, vlleh, djem, qen, cjep, krep, desh** and **presh** (Indefinite Ablative **deshësh** and **preshësh**) and **gjelazez**.

6. MPG 6: Nouns with stem ending in two consonants:

	Indefinite	Definite
Nominative	krushq	krushqit
Accusative	krushq	krushqit
Genitive	i/e krushqve	i/e krushqve
Dative	krushqve	krushqve
Ablative	krushqish/ krushqve	krushqve

7. MPG 7: Units of measurement derived from surnames, and plural stems ending in -t:

	Indefinite	Definite
Nominative	volt	voltët
Accusative	volt	voltët
Genitive	i/e voltëve	i/e voltëve
Dative	voltëve	voltëve
Ablative	voltësh/ voltëve	voltëve

Other nouns in this group include:

a. Measurements:

amper: *Ampère*, **herc**: *Hertz*, **njuton**: *Newton*, **om**: *Ohm*, **vat**: *Watt*. **Xhaul**: *joule* (plural **xhaulë**) is an exception, while **om** has an alternative form **ome**.

b. Nouns with plural stem in -**t**:

lot: *tears*, **vjet**: *years*. **Kabinet**: *cabinets* takes **e** in place of **ë**.

8. MPG 8: Substantivised adjectives. Nominative and Accusative forms are identical and therefore shown combined. Unlike nouns ending in -**t**, substantivised adjectives with stems ending in -**t** form the Definite with **it**:

a. Stem ending in -**ë** (declines as MPG 1)

	Indefinite	Definite
Nom./Acc.	**të fortë**	**të fortit**
Genitive	**i/e të fortëve**	**i/e të fortëve**
Dative	**të fortëve**	**të fortëve**
Ablative	**të fortëve/ të fortish**	**të fortëve**

b. Stem ending in unstressed vowel or in -**uj**, -**uaj**, -**iej** and -**yej** (declines as MPG 2):

	Indefinite	Definite
Nom./Acc.	**të huaj**	**të huajt**
Genitive	**i/e të huajve**	**i/e të huajve**
Dative	**të huajve**	**të huajve**
Ablative	**të huajve/ të huajsh**	**të huajve**

c. Formed from Participle (declines as MPG 4):

	Indefinite	Definite
Nom./Acc.	**të martuar**	**të martuarit**
Genitive	**i/e të martuarve**	**i/e të martuarve**
Dative	**të martuarve**	**të martuarve**
Ablative	**të martuarish/ të martuarve**	**të martuarve**

d. Single consonant stem other than -l, -r, -s, and -z (MPG 5):

	Indefinite	Definite
Nom./Acc.	**të shkathët**	**të shkathëtit**
Genitive	**i/e të shkathëtve**	**i/e të shkathëtve**
Dative	**të shkathëtve**	**të shkathëtve**
Ablative	**të shkathëtish / të shkathëtve**	**të shkathëtve**

e. Stem ending in single consonant other than -l, -r, -s and -z (MPG 5) with disappearing ë:

	Indefinite	Definite
Nom./Acc.	**të jashtëm**	**të jashtmit**
Genitive	**i/e të jashtëmve**	**i/e të jashtëmve**
Dative	**të jashtëmve**	**të jashtëmve**
Ablative	**të jashtmish/ të jashtëmve**	**të jashtëmve**

f. Stem ending in two consonants (MPG 6)

	Indefinite	Definite
Nom./Acc.	**të epërm**	**të epërmit**
Genitive	**i/e të epërmve**	**i/e të epërmve**
Dative	**të epërmve**	**të epërmve**
Ablative	**të epërmish / të epërmve**	**të epërmve**

XIV PLURAL FORMATION: MASCULINE NOUNS

1. General:

a. Masculine nouns form the plural in a variety of ways, as set out in the following paragraphs. References to the plural here are references to the Indefinite Nominative and Accusative forms. There is virtually no connection between the singular Declensions and Declension Groups on the one hand and the classification of Plural Formation Classes on the other. Some patterns can be established, but often the qualifications which have to be made merely fog the picture. Nonetheless some general principles are set out at 3. and 6. below.

b. The individual Classes are dealt with in Section XV following.

c. There is an alphabetical listing of Citation Form endings and the (Plural Formation) Classes to which they generally belong in Part F of this book. Where a noun has an ending not listed at Part F Section I, then the following guidelines may assist:

i. Animate nouns mostly form the plural with -ë.

ii. Nouns denoting inanimate objects mostly form the plural with -a, in some instances with -e.

iii. Abstract nouns most commonly form the plural with -e, thus becoming feminine in the plural.

d. The above guidelines are based on the meaning of the noun: further guidelines based on morphological factors are at 6. below.

e. The number of nouns forming the plural with the three most common endings, namely **-a**, **-e** and **-ë** (endings listed alphabetically rather than in order of frequency) is so great that it is unrealistic to try and list them. There are therefore many nouns whose CF endings do not bring them into Classes 1-12 and, because they use **-a**, **-e** or **-ë** to form the plural, they are outside the scope of this work. Many nouns can be found with more than one plural ending in everyday use

2. Principles of Classification: all references to Classes and paragraphs are to Section XV.

a. Classes 1 and 3-12 are based on the ending of the Citation Form: in Classes 6 and 7 the suffix depends, with a few exceptions, on whether the noun is animate or inanimate.

b. Class 2 contains nouns which change the stem vowel, with or without other changes.

c. Classes 13-16 comprise nouns with various CF endings, and the individual classes are based on the suffix added to form the plural.

d. Class 17 contains an assortment of nouns whose common feature is that they have alternative forms for the plural, in some instances with different meanings.

e. As in other languages there are some plural formations which defy classification. These irregular nouns are listed at Paragraph 18 of the next Section.

f. For the sake of completeness, and because they are unlikely to be found in most current dictionaries (except for **dhen**) some obsolete suppletive plurals are listed at Paragraph 19.

3. There is a large number of nouns with stem endings which do not bring them into Classes 1 or 3-12. Where the plural is formed with **-ër** or **-ra**, they are listed in the relevant Class, but those forming the plural with **-a**, **-e** and **-ë** are simply too numerous to list, forming as they do the overwhelming majority of masculine nouns. The principles at 6. below are of some help, but not infallible.

4. Relationship between MPG and Plural Classes

This paragraph deals only with the regular formations, and with major sub-groups, and references below should be interpreted in that light: to show the MPG of each irregular noun would be costly in space, and detract from the main point, which is to show the regular pattern. Nor would the user of this work wish to be spoon-fed.

Class 1	First Declension Nouns	Various
	Second Declension Nouns	MPG 3
	Third Declension Nouns	MPG 1
Class 2	Monosyllabics such as **cjep desh qen**	MPG 5
	Others	various
Class 3	Nouns with singular and plural stems ending in two consonants	MPG 6
	Other nouns forming plural with **-j**, **-gj** and **-q**	MPG 3/5
	Nouns ending in **-uj**, **-uaj**, **-iej** and **-yej**	MPG 2
	Ending in **-e**	MPG 2
Class 4	Regular formations	MPG 1
	Most exceptions	MPG 2
Class 5	Regular formations	MPG 1
	Most exceptions	MPG 2
Class 6	Animates	MPG 1

Class 6	Inanimates	MPG 2
Class 7	Animates	MPG 1
	Inanimates	MPG 2
Class 8		MPG 2
Class 9	Animates, **gram** and compounds of **gram**	MPG 1
	Others	MPG 2
Class 10		MPG 2
Class 11	Clearing house only	
Class 12		MPG 5
Class 13		MPG 5
Class 14		MPG 4
Class 15		MPG 2
Class 16		MPG 1
Class 17	By nature indefinable!	

5. Methods of formation

a. The majority adds an ending, which is often determined by the ending of the singular stem, and in some cases by the meaning of the noun – animate, substance, concrete or abstract. The commonest endings are -**a**, -**e** and -**ë**. Less common are -**ër**, -**nj** and -**ra** while a few nouns still in general use form the plural with the suffixes -**llarë** and -**lerë**. Nouns are accordingly classified below by the endings which they take in the Nominative/Accusative plural; in the majority of instances these depend on the ending of the Citation Form. There is a listing on the basis of CF endings in the Tables at Part F of this book.

b. Almost all nouns ending in -**as**, -**ës**, -**ues** and -**yes** have a plural form without suffix, thus the Nominative Indefinite Form is identical in both singular and plural.

c. Some nouns modify the stem vowel but otherwise remain unaltered.

d. Some nouns modify the final consonant of the stem and add endings.

e. Some modify the stem vowel and the final consonant, in some instances adding an ending.

f. Some are simply irregular.

g. Nouns forming the plural with the suffix **-nj** are always stressed on the final syllable in the plural. In the singular the stress in such nouns also falls on the last syllable, except for those ending in **-ua**.

h. Those nouns ending in **-n** (two listed at XV 4 d iii and six at XV 5 g) which change the final **-n** to **-nj** to form the plural are also all stressed on the final syllable.

6. The following general principles assist in determining how a masculine noun forms its plural:

a. All nouns using the suffix **-e** to form the plural become feminine in the plural and are, with very few exceptions, inanimate, and often abstract, nouns.

b. Most nouns using the suffix **-ë** to form the plural are animate: only nouns with the stress on the final syllable can take the **-ë** ending.

c. Nouns forming the plural with the suffix **-a** are almost all animate or concrete.

d. Most substance nouns, insofar as they have a plural, form this with **-ra**, and change gender. Not all nouns with this plural ending change gender.

e. Most monosyllabics add **-a** or **-ë** to form the plural.

f. Most inanimate nouns ending in **-d** or **-t** add **-e** to form the plural and therefore become feminine.

g. Polysyllabic animate nouns consisting of a stem and a (stressed) suffix generally form the plural with **-ë**.

h. The majority of the (singular) endings listed in Classes 3-8 and in Part F, are in themselves suffixes, and as such are stressed. The nouns with these endings which form apparently irregular plurals are often older words which incorporate the relevant ending as part of the stem (in contrast to a suffix).

7. Compound nouns will generally form the plural in the same way as the noun forming their second or final element: thus **kryeplak**: *village elder* forms plural **kryepleq**. Units of measurement such as **kalë-fuqi**: *horsepower* and **vit-dritë**: *light-year* form the plural by altering the first element of the compound, thus **kuaj-fuqi** and **vjet-dritë**. Likewise some compounds of **peshk**: *fish* with **peshk** as their first element.

8. Where the second element is not itself an Albanian noun, as with **aeroplan**: *aeroplane*, the other nouns with the same second element will normally follow the same pattern, particularly if the ending is one of those specified in the following section. However while **aeroplan** has the (regular) ending **-ë**, as does **hidroplan**: *hydroplane*, **biplan**: *biplane* adds **-e**. This and other irregularities in the formation of compounds are noted individually and/or in Section XXI.

9. Where nouns have alternative plural forms, these are generally set out in the relevant Class, or in the relevant Section of Part F. Class 17 therefore includes primarily those nouns which do not belong in any other Class by virtue of their stem ending.

XV MASCULINE NOUNS: CLASSES BASED ON FORMATION OF PLURAL

1. Class 1: Nouns with identical singular and plural forms.

a. This Class comprises nouns ending in **-as**, **-ës**, **-ues**, and **-yes** together with a small number of other nouns, mostly monosyllabic, with various endings, and many articulated nouns which are in fact substantivised adjectives. Nouns ending in **-as** usually denote origin or residence, while the other endings listed above generally indicate agents, instruments and utensils.

b. Nouns ending in **-as**, **-ës**, **-ues** and **-yes** have the same form in the Nominative and Accusative Plural as in the Singular, in the Indefinite Forms. Exceptions to this rule are very few, as listed below. In the Nominative and Accusative cases the number of the noun may be ascertainable from the clitic preceding any qualifying adjective, from the verb (if in the Nominative) or from the Object Clitic if in the Accusative. All other forms take the normal endings.

c. Some nouns ending in **-ër** have the same form in the Nominative and Accusative Plural as in the Singular, in the Indefinite Forms. These include **arbër**: *Albanian*, **kumtër**: *godfather* and **mjeshtër**: *master craftsman*, as well as some medical qualifications formed from the Greek root ιατηρ: *doctor* such as **psikiatër**: *psychiatrist*. A fuller list is in Part F.

d. Those Third Declension masculine nouns ending in **-ë** such as **gegë**: *Gheg* and **toskë**: *Tosk* also mostly have identical singular and plural (Nominative and Accusative Indefinite) forms. For others see Class 11.

e. Compound nouns which have as the second element an adjective ending in **-ë** such as **veshëgjatë**: *donkey* and **kryemprehtë**: *thin-lipped grey mullet* have identical singular and plural forms.

f. Nouns formed from Classical Greek or Latin and ending in **-e** such as **lice**: *lyceum* (now *middle school*) and **muze**: *museum* have identical singular and plural (Nominative and Accusative Indefinite) forms. The plural **muzeume** is sometimes seen.

g. Some other nouns likewise have identical singular and plural (Nominative and Accusative Indefinite) forms. Of these the most important are listed below, and their Definite Plural Forms are shown.

    i.   First Declension:

Indefinite: (singular and plural)	Meaning	Definite plural
ballë	*forehead*	**ballët**
dorëzanë	*guarantor*	**dorëzanët**
tru	*brain*	**trutë**
sy	*eye*	**sytë**
herc	*Hertz* (radio)	**hercët**
thopërç	*evil spirit*	**thopërçit**
muaj	*month*	**muajt**
hyj	*god*	**hyjtë**
qen	*dog*	**qentë**
shpendëkeq	*owl*	**shpendëkeqtë**
haps	*prison*	**hapsit**
presh	*leek*	**preshtë**
kabinet	*cabinet*	**kabinetet**
lot	*tear*	**lotët**
vat	*watt*	**vatët**
gjelazez	*cormorant*	**gjelazeztë**

aa. **Herc** and many other nouns derived from surnames and designating scientific units decline as set out in MPG 7 above, as do their multiples and sub-divisions. **Xhaul**: *Joule* (plural **xhaulë**) is an exception to this rule, while **om**: *Ohm* has plurals **om** or **ome**.

bb. **Peshkaqen**: *shark* forms plural **peshkaqenë**.

cc. **Presh** has Ablative plural **preshësh**.

dd. **Gjelazez** belongs to MPG 5.

    ii.   Second Declension:

mulla	*mullah*	**mullatë**
va	*ford*	**vatë**
jubile	*jubilee*	**jubiletë**
lice	*lyceum*	**licetë**
muze	*museum*	**muzetë**
trofe	*trophy*	**trofetë**
turne	*tournament*	**turnetë**
i ve/ të ve	*widower*	**të vetë**
gjeni	*genius* (person)	**gjenitë**
mazi	*oak-gall*	**mazitë**
thi	*boar*	**thitë**

    iii.   Third Declension:

dukë	*duke*	**dukët**
fëmijë	*child*	**fëmijët**
gegë	*Gheg* (person)	**gegët**
judë	*Judas, traitor*	**judët**
kallfë	*apprentice*	**kallfët**
lalë	*older person**	**lalët**
laro	*multi-coloured dog*	**larot**
palaço	*clown*	**palaçot**
qole	*servile person*	**qolet**

qose	*clean-shaven person*	**qoset**
papë	*Pope*	**papët**
toskë	*Tosk* (person)	**toskët**

h. The following are exceptions to the rule above:

i. Forming plural with **-ë**:

as	*ace* (e.g. pilot)	**kontrabas**	*double bass*
bas	*bass* (musical)	**pras**	*leek*

ii. Forming plural with **-e**:

ananas	*pineapple*	**atllas**	*satin*
as	*ace* (cards)	**hapës**	*key*
atlas	*atlas*	**ikonostas**	*iconostasis*
kompas	*compass* (geometrical)	**shkas**	*cause*
		tas	*bowl*

iii. Forming plural with **-a**:

çelës	*key*	**tas**	*crested pigeon*
dorës	see dictionary	**ujës**	*sluice gate**
gjindës	see dictionary	**zhytës**	*diver*

iv. **Udhëçelës**: *trailblazer*, arguably not a compound of **çelës**: *key*, has plural **udhëçelës**.

v. **Malazias**: *Montenegrin* forms plural **malazez**.

i. Substantivised adjectives do not alter their Indefinite Form when substantivised; thus adjectives from ADG's 1 & 2 have identical singular and plural forms apart from the preceding clitic. Examples are:

i paudhë: *the devil*, plural **të paudhë**, and **i shumëzueshëm**: *multiplier*, plural **të shumëzueshëm**.

2. Class 2: Nouns which alter the stem vowel.

a. The commonest stem vowel change between singular and plural is from **a** to **e**, which also occurs in some nouns of Class 3: the final -**a** of some nouns in Class 13 drops out before the -**enj** ending.

b. Other changes are:

i. **e** to **i**, occurring in a few Class 3 nouns.

ii. **ye** to **e**, in a few Class 3 nouns and **pëlqyer**.

iii. **ua** to **o**, in some nouns of Classes 3 and 13.

iv. **ua** to **enj** in one instance in Class 13: **përrua**.

v. Three nouns change **e** to **a**: see g ii below.

c. Class 3 nouns with vowel-stem change (**plak, lak** and **mashkull**) and some nouns ending in -**all**, -**uall** and -**yell**) are shown in that Class.

d. Nouns changing -**a** to -**e** include:

i. Without suffix:

dash	*sheep*	**desh**
cjap/sqap	*goat*	**cjep/sqep**
kulaç	*cake*	**kuleç**
krap	*carp*	**krep/krapa**
vllah	*Vlach*	**vlleh**

Dash has Ablative plural **deshësh** and its compound **deledash**: *hermaphrodite* forms plural **deledashë**.

ii. With suffix:

asht	*bone*	eshtra
atë	*father*	etër
frat	*monk*	fretër
kunat	*brother-in-law*	kunetër
lab	*Labërian*	lebër/labë
lugat	*ghost*	lugetër
malukat	*monster*	malukatë/ maluketër
mëzat	*bullock*	mëzetër
rogaç	*steer*	rogeçë
skllav	*slave*	skllevër
shtrat	*bed*	shtretër

iii. A few disyllabics alter the first vowel:

argjend	*silver*	argjende/ergjende
djalosh	*youth* (male)	djelmosha
mashkull	*man*	meshkuj

iv. The preceding consonant softens in two nouns:

ka	*ox*	qe
gardh	*fence*	gardhe/gjerdhe

e. Nouns with stem vowel **e** change as follows:

rreth	*circle**	rrethe/rrathë	17
gëthep	*hook**	gëthapë	Irregular
thes	*bag*	thasë	Irregular
breg	*hill, bank, coast*	brigje	3
shteg	*path*	shtigje	3

f. **Asht**: *plant** (**Fj.sh. s.** page 63) forms plural **ashta**.

g. **Çoban**: *shepherd* has plurals **çobanë/çobej**, the latter form being obsolete.

h. **Shpargër**: *nappy* forms plural **shpërgënj**.

3. Class 3 nouns palatalise the final consonant, in some instances adding an ending.

a. This Class comprises nouns ending in **-ll**, and nouns (mainly monosyllabic) with stems ending in **-g** and **-k**, and two nouns ending in **-r**. Those nouns formed by addition of a suffix **-ak**, **-ek**, **-ik** or **-ok** belong to Class 4 and, if irregular, are listed under that Class.

b. Masculine nouns with the following endings as a rule form the plural by palatalising the final **-ll** which thus becomes **-j**:

-all, **-uall**, **-ell**, **-iell**, **-yell**, **-ill**, **-oll** (all stressed), and **ëll** and **-ull** (unstressed).

c. Nouns with stressed stems in the singular retain that stress in the plural. Thus nouns with singular endings **-all**, **-ell**, **-ill** and **-oll** have a stressed final syllable (which is equally a syllable ending in a single consonant) and belong to MPG 3.

d. Nouns with a singular stem ending in **-uall**, **-iell** and **-yell**, where the stress is on the first letter of the diphthong, belong to MPG 2. However where the stem vowel changes in the plural to a single vowel, as **fashuall/fashoj** and **gërfyell/gërfej** the noun will belong to MPG 3. See j. below.

e. Polysyllabic nouns with a singular stem ending in **-ull**, which all have the stress on an earlier syllable, form the plural with **-uj** and belong to MPG 2.

f. Monosyllabic nouns with a singular stem ending in **-ull** are all irregular.

g. **Éngjëll**: *angel* has plural **éngjëj** (MPG 2).

h. The following drop the final **-ll** of the stem and add **-j** to form the plural. Examples: **portokall –portokaj, qiell – qiej**:

çatall	*fork*	**fëndyell**	*awl*
djall	*devil*	**fyell**	*flute**
papagall	*parrot*	**nyell**	*anklebone*
pinjall	*stiletto*	**skërfyell**	*trachea*
portokall	*orange*	**engjëll**	*angel*
buall	*buffalo, oaf*	**kërmill**	*snail*
zhguall	*shell**	**krongjill**	*icicle*
dell	*sinew*	**skundill**	*hem*
kapërcell	*pass, passage*	**thëngjill**	*coal**
kërcell	*stalk*	**ungjill**	*Gospel*
yvell	*mistletoe*	**kaproll**	*roebuck*
diell	*sun*	**akull**	*ice*
qiell	*sky*	**popull**	*people*

i. The numerous regular nouns ending in **-ull** are to be found at Part F: the following are irregular:

cull	*small boy*	**cullë**
çull	*horse blanket*	**çulle**
kull	*chestnut horse*	**kulla**
mashkull	*man*	**meshkuj**
vrull	*impetus*	**vrulle**

j. The following change stem vowels and belong to MPG 3:

CF	Meaning	Def. Sing.	Ind. Pl.
fashuall	*honeycomb*	**fasholli**	**fashoj**
gërruall	*wooden tub**	**gërrolli**	**gërroj**
gavyell	*wheel rim*	**gavelli**	**gavej**
gërbyell	*pelvic bone*	**gërbyelli**	**gërbej**
gërfyell	*tunnel*	**gërfyelli**	**gërfej**
rrëshyell	*sow-thistle*	**rrëshyelli**	**rrëshej**

k. Some nouns add **-je** in place of **-ll** and therefore become feminine. Examples: **zall – zaje, fill – fije, pyll – pyje**:

rrëzall	*dreg*	**hell**	*spit*
strall	*flint*	**fill**	*thread*
zall	*pebble**	**pyll**	*forest*

l. **Huall**: *honeycomb* and **truall**: *homeland* not only change the stem vowel but palatalise the final **-ll** and add **-e**: plurals are **hoje** and **troje**.

m. **Stërhell**: *very tall and thin person*, although animate, forms plural **stërheje**, thereby changing gender.

n. The following have alternative forms:

bakall	*grocer*	**bakej/bakaj**
çakall	*jackal*	**çakaj/çakej**
hamall	*porter**	**hamaj/hamej**
mangall	*brazier*	**mangaj/mangalle**
shuall	*sole**	**shuaj/shoje**
pinjoll	*offshoot*	**pinjollë/ pinjoj**
yll	*star*	**yje/yj**

o. Masculine nouns with the endings listed above which do not palatalise the final **-ll** are as follows:

i. Forming plural with **-ë**: example **hardall – hardallë**:

dangall	*(fat) oaf*	**kaptell**	*pommel*
hardall	*mustard*	**zgjatell**	*tall person*
mandall	*closing bar**	**bandill**	*gallant**
tellall	*town crier**	**cull**	*lad*
topall	*lame person*		

ii. Forming plural with -e: example **shall – shalle**:

fall	*fortune telling*	**prell**	*sunny place*
hall	*trouble*	**mill**	*sheath*
jambrall	*liquorice*	**trill**	*caprice*
kaçkavall	*salty ewe's milk cheese*	**protokoll**	*written record*
kapistall	*rein*	**sqoll**	*ink, basin*
kavall	*fife*	**sharapoll**	*turret**
zavall	*trouble*	**çull**	*horse blanket*
shall	*scarf*	**vrull**	*élan*

iii. **Mall**: *goods* and **miell**: *flour* form the plural with **-ra**.

iv. **Sandall**: *small boat* forms plural **sandalla**.

p. Some nouns ending in -l change this to -j:

raskal	*vine-leaf*	**raskaj**
muskul	*muscle*	**muskuj**
stimul	*stimulus*	**stimuj**

Raskal is stressed on the last syllable in both singular and plural, and the Definite plural is therefore **raskajtë**, whereas **muskul** and **stimul** have the stress on the first syllable throughout, forming Definite plural **muskujt** and **stimujt**. For other nouns ending in -**ul**, which take various plural endings, see Part F.

q. **Bir**: *son* and **lepur**: *hare, rabbit* form plurals **bij** and **lepuj**, with Definite plurals **bijtë** and **lepujt**.

r. **Krua**: *spring* and **zgjua**: *beehive* form plurals **kroje** and **zgjoje**.

s. Most monosyllabic masculine nouns ending in -**k** and -**g** palatalise the final consonant to -**q** and -**gj** respectively, as do a few other nouns with these stem endings, notably **armik**, **çiflig** and **rrezik**. A small number of nouns also changes the stem vowel.

t. A very few polysyllabic nouns ending in -**k** and -**g** also palatalise the final consonant to -**q** and -**gj** respectively, but those where -**ak**, -**ek**, -**ik** and -**ok** are suffixes form the plural by adding -**ë**.

u. Nouns which do not take an ending will belong to MPG 5 if ending in a single consonant or MPG 6 if ending in two consonants, while those which add -**e** belong to MPG 2.

v. Monosyllabic animate nouns ending in -**k** and -**g**, and also **fik** and **tirk**, change the last letter to -**q** or -**gj** respectively. Inanimate monosyllabic nouns with these endings (apart from **fik** and **tirk**) alter the final consonant and add -**e**, therefore becoming feminine in the plural. **Beng**: *golden oriole*, although animate, forms (feminine) plural **bengje**. Likewise **shtërg**: *stork* (**shtërgje**) and **molusk**: *mollusc* (**molusqe**).

w. Examples are:

   i.   Without -**e**: example **armik** – **armiq**:

armik	*enemy*	**tirk**	*man's white legging* Ø
fik	*fig*	**turk**	*Turk*
hamurik	*mole*	**visk**	*young donkey*
mik	*friend*	**krushk**	*relative by marriage**
bujk	*peasant*	**mushk**	*mule*
ujk	*wolf*	**peshk**	*fish*
ndalk	*remora, suckerfish*	**bretk**	*frog*

Ujk also has plural **ujqër**.

ii. Without -e: example: **zog – zogj**:

shtrig	*sorcerer**	**jevg**	*gypsy*
zog	*bird*	**murg**	*monk*
frëng	*Frenchman*		

Nouns with a plural stem ending in two consonants such as **ujk**, **bretk**, **jevg** and **murg** form the Definite Plural with **-it** (MPG 6) but the Definite Plural of **frëng** is **frëngjtë**.

iii. With -e: example: **cak – caqe**:

cak	*limit**	**park**	*park**
gjak	*blood feud*	**qark**	*circle**
shkak	*cause*	**qyrk**	*heavy cloak*
çek	*cheque**	**sfurk**	*pitchfork*
çelik	*steel*	**shirk**	*leather/skin*
furrik	*henhouse*		*bag*
ilik	*buttonhole*	**thark**	*weaning*
llastik	*rubber* (*tyre*)		*pen*
rrezik	*danger*	**zverk**	*nape (of*
bllok	*block*		*neck)*
çok	*knocker,*	**bisk**	*twig**
	hammer	**brisk**	*razor**
këllk	*haunch*	**disk**	*disc*
bark	*belly**	**molusk**	*mollusc*
cirk	*circus*	**dushk**	*oak**
çark	*trap**	**myshk**	*moss*
hark	*bow, curve*	**qoshk**	*kiosk*

aa. **Çek**: *Czech* forms plural **çekë**.

bb. **Gjak**: *blood* (as the substance) has plural **gjakra**.

cc. **Hark**: *bow* also has the meaning of string instrument, thus **harqet** is used to mean the String Section of an orchestra.

iv. With -e : example: **prag – pragje**:

prag	*threshold*	**beng**	*Golden Oriole**
bejleg	*duel**	**deng**	*bundle**
treg	*market*	**peng**	*pledge*
çiflig	*estate*	**rreng**	*dirty trick*
navig	*doorbolt*	**lëng**	*juice*
vig	*stretcher*	**plëng**	*worldly goods, hearth and home*
fushlog	*village square*		
log	*clearing*	**miting**	*meeting*
plog	*haystack*	**parking**	*car park*
prog	*hobnail*	**ring**	*(boxing) ring*
shtog	*elderberry tree*	**diftong**	*diphthong*
tog	*group, platoon*	**cung**	*(tree) stump*
lug	*trough*	**trung**	*trunk**
plug	*plough*	**qyng**	*pipe, duct*
zdrug	*plane*	**varg**	*row, series*
shelg	*willow*	**fërg**	*frying-pan*
pellg	*pool, basin**	**shtërg**	*stork*
fang	*sod (of earth)*	**pirg**	*tower**
rang	*rank*	**çurg**	*trickle*
vang	*wheelrim*	**vurg**	*boggy ground*
aheng	*revelry*		

x. Four nouns also change the stem vowel:

breg	*coast**	**brigje**
shteg	*path**	**shtigje**
lak	*loop**	**leqe**
plak	*old man*	**pleq**

y. Nouns ending in **-llëk** change the final **-k** to **-q** and add **-e**:

budallallëk	nonsense	budallallëqe
çilimillëk	prank*	çilimillëqe
matrapazllëk	dirty business	matrapazllëqe
pazarllëk	haggling	pazarllëqe
tarafllëk	cronyism	tarafllëqe

z. Some nouns ending in -ak, -ek, -ëk, -ik, -uk and -yk have two plural forms; either -ë is added to the stem, or the -k is palatalised to -q and -e added. However this is not so when the endings above are in fact part of a longer suffix. Thus nouns ending in -nik, such as **vajnik**: *oilcan* and **vërsnik**: *person of the same age* form plural only with -kë. It will be seen from the list below that nearly all the nouns with alternative plural forms are disyllabic. An example is as follows:

bajrak: *flag*, plurals **bajrakë** and **bajraqe**.

bajrak	flag	dyfek	rifle
hak	revenge	dyshek	mattress
oxhak	chimney	hendek	ditch
qorrsokak	cul-de-sac	jastëk	pillow
sanxhak	Ottoman province	sarëk	turban
		ibrik	kettle
shtrak	skin, carpel	gërtuk	see dictionary
byrek	pastry	muslluk	spigot, tap

Gjyslykë and **gjyslyke** are alternative (plural only) forms meaning *spectacles*.

aa. The following nouns do not palatalise the final consonant and form the plural with -ë:

i. Monosyllabic ending in -g:

belg	Belgian	erg	erg
eng	deaf-mute	morg	morgue

ii. Monosyllabic ending in -k:

flok	*hair*	**krik**	*jack* (for vehicle)
frak	*frock-coat*	**lek**	*Lek* (currency)
gjok	*gray* (white horse)	**mjek**	*doctor* (medical)
jak	*yak*	**shok**	*friend*

iii. Polysyllabics ending in -g or -k:

kuisling	*collaborator*	**smoking**	*dinner-jacket*
çerek	*quarter*	**zambak**	*lily*
lejlek	*stork*		

Also formations from Greek roots such as **stomatolog**: *dentist*.

bb. The following nouns do not palatalise the final consonant and form the plural with **-e**:

merak	*concern*	**dok**	*dock*
ngjak	*blood clot*	**kalk**	*tracing paper*
tiktak	*tick-tock*	**gong**	*gong*

cc. The following nouns form the plural with **-a**:

i. Ending in **-g**:

frang   *Franc* (Swiss currency) **franga**

ii. Ending in **-k**:

çik	*hint*	**çika**
shuk	*wad*	**shuka**
petk	*cloak*	**petka**

Petk was formerly neuter, and the plural **petka** is feminine.

4. **Class 4 nouns add -ë to form the plural.**

a. This Class comprises nouns ending in suffixes **-ac, -aç, -af, -ak, -aq, -ash, -eç, -ek, -en, -esh, -ik, -in, -ist, -jan, -jot, -ok, -or, -osh, -ot, -tar, -tor** and **-uk**. With these nouns the stress is on the suffix, and the plural is formed with **-ë**. When used as adjectives they also take this ending in the masculine plural.

b Only polysyllabic nouns with the above endings, where the last syllable is a suffix, follow this rule, since in monosyllabic nouns the ending is, for example, **-k** rather than **-ak, -ek, -ik** or **-ok**. Monosyllabic nouns ending in **-k** are listed under Class 3. It follows that the apparent exceptions to the rule above are in many instances monosyllabic.

c. Examples of nouns with the above suffixes are:

Ending	Noun	Meaning	Plural
-ac	**koprrac**	*miser*	**koprracë**
-aç	**gjembaç**	*thistle*	**gjembaçë**
-af	**paragraf**	*paragraph*	**paragrafë**
-ak	**binjak**	*twin*	**binjakë**
-aq	**shkataraq**	*slovenly person*	**shkataraqë**
-ash	**gjumash**	*sleepyhead*	**gjumashë**
-eç	**kryeneç**	*stubborn person*	**kryeneçë**
-ek	**fishek**	*cartridge*	**fishekë**
-en	**kapiten**	*captain*	**kapitenë**
-esh	**arbëresh**	*Arbëresh*	**arbëreshë**
-ik	**akademik**	*academician*	**akademikë**
-in	**pinguin**	*penguin*	**pinguinë**
-ist	**futbollist**	*footballer*	**futbollistë**
-jan	**lumjan**	*Inhabitant of Lumë*	**lumjanë**
-jot	**himarjot**	*Inhabitant of Himarë*	**himarjotë**
-ok	**maçok**	*tomcat*	**maçokë**

-or	**banor**	*resident*	**banorë**
-osh	**trimosh**	*lad*	**trimoshë**
-ot	**patriot**	*patriot*	**patriotë**
-tar	**shkrimtar**	*writer*	**shkrimtarë**
-tor	**murator**	*bricklayer*	**muratorë**
-uk	**bishtuk**	*oil lamp*	**bishtukë**

d. Exceptions are:

i. Ending in -**a**:

dac	*tomcat*	**fren**	*brake*
gurgac	*flint*	**qepen**	*trap door*
armaç	*brocade strip*	**raven**	*rhubarb*
baç	*strap, belt**	**tren**	*train*
gaç	*donkey colt*	**kaloshin**	*gig* (carriage)
gërraç	*hooked stick*	**puplin**	*poplin*
kësaç	*pliers*	**temin**	*bauble*
gjeldash	*hoopoe**	**kosh**	*basket*
beden	*bulwark*	**belot**	see dictionary

ii. Ending in -**e**:

biraç	*fireside niche*	**plaf**	*horse blanket*
haraç	*tribute payable*	**taraf**	*faction*
ilaç	*medicine*	**mjerak**	*woe*
laç	*wetland*	**ngjak**	*blood clot*
maç	*Spades* (cards)	**tiktak**	*ticking*
saç	*Dutch oven*	**tallash**	*shavings, sawdust*
taç	see dictionary	**telash**	*trouble, clash*
trokaç	*cowbell*	**skeç**	*sketch*
af	*sheen*	**cen**	*defect*
autograf	*autograph*	**fenomen**	*phenomen*
epitaf	*epitaph*	**gjen**	*gene*
esnaf	*guild*	**liken**	*lichen*
llaf	*chat, word*	**liqen**	*lake*
peshtaf	*jewellery box*	**nen**	*clause* (legal)

refren	*refrain*	**kor**	*choir*
terren	*terrain*	**korridor**	*corridor*
rrebesh	*downpour*	**plor**	*ploughshare*
buletin	*bulletin*	**por**	*pore**
cist	*cyst*	**tumor**	*tumour*
kist	*interest payment*	**llosh**	*see dictionary*
		varosh	*suburb*
shist	*schist*	**fokstrot**	*foxtrot*
dekor	*decoration*	**komplot**	*plot*
favor	*favour*	**mot**	*weather*

iii. Other plural forms:

kulaç	*cake*	**kuleç**
rogaç	*steer*	**rogeçë**
dash	*ram*	**desh**
bërshen	*English yew*	**bërshenj**
qen	*dog*	**qen**
lesh	*hair, wool*	**leshra**
kulmetin	*water poplar*	**kulmetinj**
armik	*enemy*	**armiq**
fik	*fig*	**fiq**
mik	*friend*	**miq**
djalosh	*lad*	**djelmosha**
lot	*tear*	**lot**
zot	*God*	**zota**
zot	*master*	**zotërinj**

e. Monosyllabic nouns ending in **-ak**, **-ek**, **-ik** or **-ok**, such as **mik**, are listed in Class 3.

f. **Peshkaqen**: *shark/dogfish* forms plural **peshkaqenë**.

g. **Llosh** has an alternative plural **lloshra**: *trash*.

5. <u>Class 5 nouns mostly add - **ë** to form the plural.</u>

a. This Class comprise nouns ending in -**an**, -**ar**, -**ec**, -**er**, -**ir**, -**ol**, -**on** (except those ending in - **ion**) and -**un**.

b. The majority of nouns of this Class adds -**ë** to form the plural, as for example:

-**an**	**politikan**	*politician*	**politikanë**
-**ar**	**kalendar**	*calendar*	**kalendarë**
-**ec**	**memec**	*deafmute*	**memecë**
-**er**	**shofer**	*driver*	**shoferë**
-**ir**	**zinxhir**	*chain*	**zinxhirë**
-**ol**	**kaqol**	*walnut**	**kaqolë**
-**on**	**vagon**	*railway wagon*	**vagonë**
-**un**	**majmun**	*monkey*	**majmunë**

c. There are, however, numerous exceptions, some of which form the plural with -**a**, and some with -**e**. These lists make no claim to be comprehensive, but the most commonly found are:

d. Forming plural with -**a**:

-**an**	**kreshtan**	(*large-combed*) *rooster*	**kreshtana**
	man	*mulberry*	**mana**
	patëllxhan	*aubergine*	**patëllxhana**
-**ec**	**bec**	*young lamb*	**beca**
	bishtalec	*pigtail*	**bishtaleca**
	gërdec	*kidney-vetch**	**gërdeca**
	gërrec	*socket*	**gërreca**
	gogëlec	*white fig*	**gogëleca**
	karkalec	*grasshopper*	**karkaleca**
	kastravec	*cucumber*	**kastraveca**
	kec	(*goat*) *kid*	**keca/kecër**
	spec	(*red*) *pepper*	**speca**

-er	gjer	*dormouse*	gjera
-ol	bobol	*nettle-tree*	bobola
	bombol	*cylinder*	bombola
	gol	*goal*	gola
	portofol	*briefcase*	portofola
	qafol	*horse-collar*	qafola
	sokol	*falcon*	sokola
	spol	*scoop, bailer*	spola
	stol	*stool*	stola
	xhol	*Joker* (cards)	xhola
-on	bulon	*bolt*	bulona
	gramafon	*gramophone*	gramafona
	kupon	*coupon*	kupona
	magnetofon	*tape-recorder*	magnetofona
	mikrofon	*microphone*	mikrofona
	person	*person*	persona
	piston	*piston*	pistona
	telefon	*telephone*	telefona
	napolon	*Napoleon (coin)*	napolona
-un	çun	*lad*	çuna
	zhgun	*woollen fabric**	zhguna

e. Other nouns of foreign origin ending in **-fon** also form the plural with **-a**, except for **ksilofon**: *xylophone* (plural **ksilofonë**) and **radiogramafon**: *radiogram* (plural **radiogramafonë**).

f. Forming plural with **-e** and therefore becoming feminine (all inanimate except **bakter** and **kurban**):

i. Ending in **-an**: example **plan** – **plane**:

aranzhman	*package holiday*		
bezistan	*covered market*		
biplan	*biplane*	**divan**	*divan*
bostan	*melon**	**duhan**	*tobacco*
derman	*remedy*	**dyqan**	*shop*

ekran	*screen*	**saftjan**	*morocco**
fustan	*dress*	**savan**	*shroud*
han	*roadside shelter**	**slogan**	*slogan*
kurban	*sacrificial animal, scapegoat*	**stan**	*flock**
		tavan	*ceiling*
liman	*harbour*	**timpan**	*eardrum*
mejdan	*battlefield*	**tufan**	*storm*
oqean	*ocean*	**uragan**	*hurricane*
organ	*organ*	**vullkan**	*volcano*
plan	*plan*	**zhgan**	*mob, pack*

Aeroplan and **hidroplan** form the plural with -**ë**.

ii. Ending in -**ar**: example **pazar** – **pazare**:

far	*lighthouse*	**trotuár**	*pavement*
jar	*see dictionary*	**thesar**	*treasure**
pazar	*market*	**visar**	*treasure*
seminar	*seminar**	**zar**	*die* (single of "dice")
tipar	*feature*	**zarar**	*damage*

The second vowel of the diphthong is stressed in **trotuár**.

iii. Ending in -**ec**: **kotec**: *hencoop*.

iv. Ending in -**er**: example: **ylber** – **ylbere**:

bakter	*bacterium*	**kriter**	*criterion*
ber	*arc*	**liker**	*liqueur*
dikaster	*ministry*	**minder**	*bench*
eter	*ether*	**mister**	*mystery*
haber	*news*	**qer**	*pastry board*
karakter	*character*	**ylber**	*rainbow*
krater	*crater*	**zeher**	*poison*

v. Ending in **-ir**: example **panair – panaire**:

gjir	*whirlpool*	**panair**	*fair*
hir	*kindness**	**sehir**	*stare*
manastir	*monastery*	**xhevahir**	*diamond*

vi. Ending in **-ol**: example **symbol – simbole**:

arkivol	*coffin*	**metropol**	*metropolis*
cikol	*small peak*	**mol**	*mole*(nautical)
gjol	*marsh*	**monopol**	*monopoly*
karambol	*carom, collision*	**pol**	*Pole* (geog)
		simbol	*symbol*

vii. Ending in **-on**: example **shabllon – shabllone**:

ballkon	*balcony*	**kon**	*cone*
ciklon	*cyclone*	**neutron**	*neutron*
diapazon	*diapason*	**pavijon**	*pavilion*
elektron	*electron*	**poligon**	*training area, range (military)*
fejton	*feuilleton*		
fron	*throne*		
garnizon	*garrison*	**proton**	*proton*
hon	*gorge*	**sallon**	*hall*
hormon	*hormone*	**sifon**	*siphon*
ipsilon	*upsilon*	**shabllon**	*template*
jon	*ion*	**zakon**	*custom*
kanton	*canton*	**zhargon**	*jargon*

viii. Ending in **-un**:

bun	*shepherd's hut*	**bune**
cibun	*white flannel cape*	**cibune**
kanun	*Legal Code*	**kanune**
tajfun	*typhoon*	**tajfune**

g. A few nouns with the endings above form the plural by altering the final -**n** of the stem to -**nj**. These include **bërcan**: *big olive*, **carian**: *hearthstone*, **gocan**: *pumice-stone*, **rruvan**: *grape-stalk*, **vidan**: *(male) pigeon* and **barbun**: *red mullet*. The final syllable of these nouns is stressed both in the singular and plural.

h. **Hajvan**: *beast of burden* has an alternative plural **hajvanër** when used figuratively.

i. **Çoban**: *shepherd* has plurals **çobanë/çobej**, the latter form being obsolete.

j. **Bar**: *grass* forms plural **barëra** while **bar**: *medicine* forms plural **barna**, which may be feminine. Their homonyms **bar**: *bar* and **bar**: *Bar* (unit of air pressure) form plural **barë**.

k. **Buburrec**: *bug* has plurals **buburrecë/ buburreca**.

l. **Bir**: *son* forms plural **bij**.

m. **Pëlqyer** (Def. **pëlqeri**) : *thumb* forms plural **pëlqerë**.

n. **Ton** has various meanings. It forms a regular plural **tonë** but **ton**: *tone* forms plural **tone.**

o. **Pirun**: *fork* has a regular plural **pirunë** and an alternative plural **pirunj** which is not listed in **Fjalor sh.s**. So does **spiun**: *spy*.

6. Class 6: Nouns with plural suffixes dependent on meaning: **-ë** when they denote animate beings, and **-e** when they denote inanimate objects or are abstract nouns.

a. This Class comprise nouns with the endings **-al, -ant, -at, -az, -el, -ent, -et, -ez, -id, -ier/-jer,- it** and **-ont**.

b. Examples are:

Singular	Meaning	Plural
intelektual	*intellectual*	**intelektualë**
lokal	*premises*	**lokale**
kursant	*student*	**kursantë**
diamant	*diamond*	**diamante**
diplomat	*diplomat*	**diplomatë**
agregat	*generator*	**agregate**
matrapaz	*black-marketeer*	**matrapazë**
kafaz	*cage**	**kafaze**
kriminel	*criminal*	**kriminelë**
hotel	*hotel*	**hotele**
student	*student*	**studentë**
dokument	*document*	**dokumente**
deputet	*Member of Parliament*	**deputetë**
fakultet	*faculty*	**fakultete**
berlinez	*Berliner*	**berlinezë**
trapez	*trapezoid*	**trapeze**
invalid	*disabled person*	**invalidë**
oksid	*oxide*	**okside**
inxhinier	*engineer*	**inxhinierë**
kantier	*work yard*	**kantiere**
petrit	*falcon*	**petritë**
suficit	*surplus*	**suficite**
rinoqeront	*rhinoceros*	**rinoqerontë**
horizont	*horizon*	**horizonte**

c. Some inanimate nouns form the plural with -**ë**: example **kuintal** – **kuintalë**:

kuintal	*quintal (100 Kg)*	**testembel**	*knucklebone**
tropal	*boulder*	**cent**	*cent*
altoparlant	*loudspeaker*	**precedent**	*precedent*
desant	*assault troops*	**planet**	*planet*
automat	*machine**	**diez**	*sharp* (musical)
karat	*carat*	**lez**	*wart*
kilovat	*Kilowatt*	**dolomit**	*dolomite*
dhiqel	*hoe, dibble*	**meit**	*corpse*
kokoçel	*cornflower*	**meteorit**	*meteorite*
paralel	*parallel*	**satelit**	*satellite*

d. Some inanimate nouns form the plural with -**a**:

bat	*bird-trap*	**tel**	*wire**
shat	*hoe*	**vel**	*sail*
thumbat	*wooden pin*	**violonçel**	*cello*
shatërkaz	*Dutch hoe*	**zhamel**	*boulder*
bel	*spade*	**briket**	*briquette*
çengel	*hook**	**gërshet**	*hair braid*
penel	*paintbrush*	**koret**	*skirt**
shrapnel	*shrapnel round*	**brez**	*belt**
tegel	*seam*	**shirit**	*tape**

e. These inanimate nouns have alternative plurals:

gërxhel	*tree stump*	**gërxhela/ gërxhelë**
reçel	*jam*	**reçele/ reçelra**
mret	*mock privet*	**mrete/mreta**

f. The following animate nouns are irregular:

gjelazez	Class 1	*cormorant*	**gjelazez**
fant	Class 6	*knave* (cards)	**fante**
bubazhel	Class 6	*larva*	**bubazhela**

gjel	Class 6	*rooster*	**gjela**
harabel	Class 6	*sparrow*	**harabela**
kalëdet	Class 8	*seahorse*	**kalëdete**
personalitet	Class 8	*personality*	**personalitete**
dhaskal	Class 13	*pedant, ineffective teacher*	**dhaskenj**
mbret	Class 14	*king*	**mbretër**
at	Class 16	*saddle horse*	**atllarë**

g. The following inanimate nouns are irregular:

vat	Class 1	*watt*	**vat**
kabinet	Class 1	*cabinet*	**kabinet**
raskal	Class 3	*vine-leaf*	**raskaj**
fshat	Class 15	*village*	**fshatra**
gaz	Class 15	*gas*	**gaze/gazra**
bulmet	Class 15	*dairy product*	**bulmetra**
vit	Class 17	*year*	**vite/vjet**

h. **Frat, kunat, lugat, mëzat** and **shtrat** form the plurals in **-etër** and belong in Class 2. Likewise **malukat**, which has plurals **malukatë /maluketër**.

i. See Class 15 for notes on the gender of **fshatra**.

j. **Gaz**: *pleasure* forms plural **gaze**.

k. **Kundërgaz**: *gas mask* forms plural **kundërgaze**.

l. **Bel**: *spade* forms plural **bela** while **bel**: *waist* forms plural **bele**.

m. **Element**: *element* has two plural forms, **elemente** meaning *chemical elements* and **elementë** meaning *persons* as in **elementë marksistë**: *Marxist elements*.

n. **Parazit**: *parasite* (plural **parazitë**) is animate!

7. Class 7: Nouns ending in -**il** and -**oz**.

a. Similarly to Class 6 these nouns have different plural endings for animate and inanimate nouns. Animate nouns with these endings form the plural with -**ë**, and inanimate nouns with -**a**:

civil	*civilian*	**civilë**
trëndafil	*rose*	**trëndafila**
tifoz	*enthusiast*	**tifozë**
kavanoz	*glass jar*	**kavanoza**

b. Exceptions are:

i. Inanimate nouns forming plural with -**ë**. Example **cimbil** - **cimbilë**:

cimbil	*goad, awl*	**petrahil**	*stole*
daktil	*dactyl* (verse measure)	**topil**	*reservoir*
		zhabil	*buttercup*

ii. Nouns (inanimate except **bacil**) forming plural with -**e** and becoming feminine. Example **bacil** - **bacile**:

azil	*old people's home*	**kadril**	*quadrille*
bacil	*bacillus*	**profil**	*profile*
fosil	*fossil*	**stil**	*style*
idil	*idyll*	**tekstil**	*textile*
lloz	*bolt*	**toz**	*powder*
patoz	*area of trampled earth*		

c. **Bilbil**: *nightingale* is also used with the meaning of *whistle* (musical instrument). In both meanings it forms the plural **bilbila**. Likewise **fil**: *elephant* and **fil**: *guardrail* both form plural **fila**.

d. **Trishtil**: *tit* (ornithological: *parus*) has plural **trishtila**.

8. Class 8: Nouns ending in **-azh, -ezh, -ël, -im, -ion, -(i)um, -ozh** and **-us** and forming the plural with **-e**.

a. This Class comprises Masculine nouns with the above endings, most of which are abstract, and all of which require the plural ending **-e,** and also includes the animate nouns **bacil, bakter, insekt, mikrob, personalitet** and **virus.**

b. These nouns are almost always inanimate, and mostly abstract, and become feminine in the plural. Those with the above endings which add a suffix other than **-e** do not change gender.

c. Examples are:

ambalazh	*packaging*	**ambalazhe**
kortezh	*cortege*	**kortezhe**
vendim	*decision*	**vendime**
profesion	*profession*	**profesione**
stadium	*stadium*	**stadiume**
elozh	*elogy*	**elozhe**

d. The following, many of which are animate, take endings other than **-e**, and therefore remain masculine in the plural:

i. Ending in **-a:** example **trim – trima**:

curlimim	*twittering*	**trim**	*brave person*
qilim	*carpet*		

ii. Ending in **-ë:** example **avion - avionë**:

anonim	*anonymous person*	**gjeneralisim**	*generalissimo*
		jetim	*orphan*

avion	*aeroplane*	**mikrobus**	*minibus*
kamion	*lorry*	**obus**	*howitzer*
autobus	*bus*	**trolejbus**	*trolleybus*

e. The following animate nouns form the plural with **-e**:

Noun	Cl.	Meaning	Noun	Cl.	Meaning
bacil	7	*bacillus*	**mikrob**	-	*microbe*
bakter	5	*bacterium*	**personalitet**	6	*personality*
insekt	-	*insect*	**personazh**	8	*person*
kalëdet	6	*seahorse*	**virus**	8	*virus*

Class 3 animates which become feminine in the plural are listed in Class 3 and at Part XXIV.

f. **Kampion** has alternative plural forms:

kampionë: *champions* and **kampione**: *samples.*

g. **Milion**: *million* has plurals **milionë** and **miliona**: see Class 17. The meanings of **bilion** and **trilion** (both of which form the plural with **-ë**) are discussed in Part D.

h. **Llum**: *sludge* forms plural **llumra**.

i. Many other inanimate nouns, with endings not listed among the Class headings set out here, form the plural with **-e**. From the selection below it can be seen that while the **-e** ending is generally associated with abstract nouns, there are also many concrete nouns with this plural ending. Examples: **fis – fise**:

fis	*clan*	**gjynah**	*sin*
flaut	*flute*	**haúz**	*pond*
gjiriz	*sewer*	**hesap**	*account*
gjoks	*chest*	**lloj**	*variety, type*

9. <u>Class 9: Nouns ending in -**am**</u>.

a. Nouns ending in -**am,** which are almost all of foreign origin, fall into two main groups:

i. **Gram:** *gramme* and its compounds denoting units of weight such as **kilogram** form the plural with -**ë** as in **gramë, kilogramë**.

ii. Nouns formed from the Greek root γραμ: *writing* form the plural in -**e,** and become feminine, as **diagram/ diagrame:** *diagram*, **pentagram/pentagrame**: (musical) *stave*, **telegram/ telegrame** *telegram*.

b. The following are outside the above categories:

i. Animate nouns forming plural with -**ë**: example **imam** – **imamë**:

Çam	*native of Chameria*	**nizam**	*nizam* (soldier in Ottoman
hipopotam	*hippopotamus*		Army)
imam	*imam*	**vëllam**	*best man*

Çam: *native of Chameria* has alternative plural **Çamër,** while **çam:** *silver fir* forms plural **çame**.

ii. Inanimate nouns forming plural with -**a**: example **xham** – **xhama**. However **xham** also has a regular plural **xhame**.

kallam   *reed**   **xham**   *(pane of) glass*

10. <u>Class 10: Nouns ending in **-ël**, **-izëm**, **-ër**, **-ul** and **-ur** and forming plural with **-a**.</u>

a. This Class comprises:

i. A small number of masculine nouns ending in **-ël**, which drop the **ë** of the Citation Form in declension.

ii. **Prizëm**: *prism* and those nouns ending in **-izëm** which have plural forms, and likewise drop the **ë** of the CF in declension, e.g. **prizma**, **aforizma**: *aphorisms*.

iii. Most (masculine) nouns ending in **-ër**, which drop the **ë** of the Citation Form in declension, e.g. **emër**: *name*, plural **emra**. The most commonly found of these nouns, together with exceptions, are listed at Part F. This sub-class includes **metër** and **litër** and their multiples and sub-units, together with **filtër.** It also includes instruments with **-metër** as the second element, whereas agent nouns with **-metër** and **-iatër** as their second element have Nominative Plural Indefinite Forms identical to the CF.

iv. Some (masculine) nouns ending in **-ul**, as listed at Part F.

v. A very few nouns ending in **-ur** with the stress on the penultimate syllable, as listed at Part F: note that **lepur** belongs to Class 3.

vi. **Qehën**: *baker's shovel* (plural **qehna**) and **zgjebëç**: *clematis* (plural **zgjebça**) decline in similar fashion.

vii. There are additionally many one- and two-syllable nouns, with a wide variety of CF endings, denoting animate beings or concrete objects which form the plural with **-a**. Examples **burrë - burra**, **hut - huta**:

bërryl	*elbow*	iç	*pastry filling*
bisht	*tail*	interes	*motive*
burrë	*man, husband*	korb	*raven*
dem	*calf*	lis	*oak*
derr	*pig*	morr	*louse*
fatos	*hero*	person	*person*
filiz	*sapling*	pëllumb	*dove*
film	*film*	plep	*poplar*
gic	*(wild piglet)*	plumb	*bullet*
gol	*goal*	qilim	*carpet*
gjel	*type of water fowl*	shef	*boss*
gjer	*dormouse*	top	*large gun*
horr	*rascal*	trup	*body*
hut	*hoot owl*	tub	*tube*

b. Although many nouns in this Class have plurals ending with the letters **ra**, the **r** forms part of the stem; they are therefore correctly described as ending in -**a**.

c. **Ansambël**: *ensemble*, **biçikël**: *bicycle* and **cikël**: *cycle* form plurals **ansamble**, **biçikle** and **cikle** respectively. **Triçikël**: *tricycle* forms plural **triçikla**.

d. The following nouns ending in -**ër** have irregular plurals:

bakër	*copper (goods)*	bakra/bakëre
drapër	*sickle*	drapinj/drapërinj
dhëndër	*son-in-law*	dhëndurë
gjarpër	*snake*	gjarpinj/gjarpërinj
hatër	*favour*	hatëre
kinoteatër	*cinema/ theatre*	kinoteatro
kuadër	*framework, personnel*	kuadro
satër	*meat-cleaver*	satëre
shpargër	*nappy*	shpërgënj
talër	*open vat*	talëre
teatër	*theatre*	teatra/teatro

e. **Shul**: *pole, perch, pivot* has plural forms **shule** and **shula**.

f. **Hekur**: *iron* and **pluhur**: *dust* form plurals **hekura** and **pluhura** respectively. **Hekura** means *iron goods* as in **hekurat e frerit**: *the bit* (of a bridle) while **pluhura** means *quantities of dust* as in **pluhurat e rrugës**: *the dust of the road*. These shifts in meaning are similar to those of other substance nouns.

g. Nouns ending in **-ël, -izëm, -ër, -ul** and **-ur**, both regular and irregular, are listed at Part F, Section VII.

h. The following nouns, although not having the endings quoted above, are mentioned elsewhere in other Classes:

i. **Zë**, which extends the stem to **zër-** retains this stem extension in the plural form **zëra**. Similarly **hi**: *ash* forms plural **hira**. **Dry**: *padlock* retains the stem extension **-n** to form plural **dryna**.

ii. **Bar** with the meaning of *medicine* forms plural **barna** which may be feminine.

iii. **Bacë**, which is used to denote male relatives and as a term of respect, forms plural **baca**.

i. **Edh**: *goat-kid*, **qengj**: *lamb* and **viç**: *calf* form the plural with **-a**: obsolete suppletive forms are shown in Paragraph 19 of this section.

j. The abbreviation **VIP**: *VIP* forms plural **VIP-a**, taking the plural form from **persona**, as in:.

Saranda, aty ku pushojnë VIP-at e politikës: *Saranda, where the VIP's of politics holiday.*

11. Class 11: Nouns ending in unstressed -ë.

a. Masculine nouns ending in unstressed -ë take a variety of plural endings: all are therefore in other Classes. This Class is not so much a Class as a Clearing House.

b. Third Declension masculine nouns with this ending are mostly in Classes 1 and 16, and are listed at XI 4 d.

c. The following (formerly neuter) substance nouns form the plural with -ra and belong in Class 15:

brumë	*dough*	**gjalpë**	*butter*
djathë	*cheese*	**mjaltë**	*honey*
drithë	*grain*	**ujë**	*water*
dhjamë	*tallow*		

d. Other plural formations are as follows:

atë	*father*	**etër**
ballë	*forehead*	**ballë**
burrë	*man, husband*	**burra**
djalë	*lad*	**djem**
kalë	*horse*	**kuaj**
lëmë	*work area*	**lëmenj**
lumë	*river*	**lumenj**

120

12. **Class 12. Nouns ending in stressed vowel.**

a. This Class comprises masculine nouns ending in stressed **-e**, **-ë**, **-i**, **-o** or **-u**, including monosyllabics, and a small number of nouns ending in stressed **-a**. Apart from **vëlla**, which is irregular, most other nouns ending in stressed **-a** are in Class 16. Most nouns in this Class form the plural with **-nj**, and the final syllable (ending in **-nj**) is always stressed. The second group in terms of size forms the plural with **-rë** and there are a few irregular formations. Those nouns which take a further or different vowel before the ending are in Class 13. The class includes nouns of Turkish origin such as **bakllavxhi**: *baklava maker*, **sahatçi**: *watchmaker* and **qejfli** *fast-living person*.

b. Nouns forming the plural with **-nj** are as follows:

i. First Declension with **-ri** stem extension in singular. This extension is dropped and **-nj** added. Example: **hu – hunj**:

gdhe	*black pine**	**arti**	*Heldreich pine*
kacadre	*stag beetle*	**flori**	*florin**
pe	*thread*	**fulqi**	*jaw*
vgje	*Austrian pine*	**gji**	*breast*
mëllë	*see dictionary*	**kalli**	*ear of corn**
kërci	*shinbone*	**shalqi**	*water melon*
kërthi	*suckling**	**turi**	*snout*
kushëri	*cousin*	**ulli**	*olive*
mulli	*mill*	**hu**	*post, stake*
pëqi	*lap*	**kërcu**	*tree stump*
qiri	*candle*		

aa. **Dru**: *tree* (**druri**) has the plural form **drurë**: **drunj** is the plural of the feminine noun **dru**: *firewood*.

bb. **Gju**: *knee* (**gjuri**) has plural **gjunjë**, Definite plural **gjunjët**.

ii. First Declension extending the stem with **-ni**. The stem extension is dropped and **-nj** added. Example **bli/blinj**:

kacara	*cudgel*	buli	*water elm*
vulla	*strip of land*	ulpëti	*wych elm*
arne	*Heldreich pine*	galacu	*paralytic*
bli	*sturgeon*	kacabu	*cockroach*

iii. First Declension without stem extension:

| afendiko (i) | *see dictionary* | afendikonj |
| hero (i) | *hero* | heronj |

iv. Second Declension. Example: **bari – barinj**:

farise	*Pharisee*	bari	*shepherd*
hebre	*Hebrew*	borxhli	*debtor*
lake	*lackey*	çilimi	*child*
pigme	*pygmy*	deli	*hero*
ari	*bear*	kapadai	*bully*
axhami	*child*	qejfli	*fun-lover*
komshi	*neighbour*	qiraxhi	*hirer, tenant*
kryemyfti	*chief mufti*	sahatçi	*watchmaker*
mi	*mouse*	terzi	*tailor**
myfti	*mufti*	zanatçi	*craftsman*
myshteri	*customer*	zhapi	*green lizard*

v. Third Declension: **zotëri**: *master*, **jeremi**: *hermit*.

vi. **Myfti** has alternative plural **myftilerë**: **kryemufti**: *chief mufti* has only the form **kryemyftinj**.

vii. **Këmishëzi** has plurals **këmishëzinj** and **këmishëzezë**.

c. Nouns forming the plural by retaining the -**r** stem extension and adding -**ë** are as follows: Example **dru** / **drurë**:

kryetra	*lintel*	**bri**	*horn*
tra	*beam*	**dru**	*tree, wood*
dre	*deer*	**mëru**	*handle for blade*
fre	*bridle, rein*	**sqepadru**	*woodpecker*
bli	*lime tree*		

d. Nouns with identical singular and plural forms are:

i. First Declension:

hu/huni	see dictionary	**hu**
tru/truri	*brain*	**tru**
sy/syri	*eye*	**sy**

ii. Second Declension:

mulla	*mullah*	**turne**	*tournament*
va	*ford*	**mazi**	*oak-gall*
jubile	*jubilee*	**thi**	*boar*
trofe	*trophy*		

e. **Aga, baba, usta** and **xhaxha** form the plural with -**llarë**. (Class 16).

f. **Bej** (singular stem **be-**), **haxhi, kadi** and **myfti** form the plural with -**lerë**. (Class 16).

g. The following form the plural by adding -**j** to the CF. Since the final syllable is stressed, the normal ending for the Definite plural is -**të** (MPG 3). However **kalama** and **mëti** form the Definite plural with -**t**:

i. First Declension (-**ri** extension):

kufi	*border*	**kufij**

ii.　First Declension (**-ni** extension):

kalama	*child**	**kalamaj**
rogja	*branch of delta*	**rogjaj**
mëti	churn	**mëtij**

iii.　Second Declension:

ble	*volume* (of book)	**blej**
derebe	*Ottoman feudal official*	**derebej**

h.　Other plural formations are as follows:

　　i.　First Declension (Group 4):

vëlla	*brother*	**vëllezër**

　　ii.　First Declension (**-ri** extension):

mëllë	see dictionary	**mëllënj**
shullë	*sunny place*	**shullëre**
zë	*voice*	**zëra**
hi	*ash*	**hira**
tru	*brain*	**tru**
sy	*eye*	**sy**

Zë forms the plural by adding **-a** to the extended stem **zër-**, and therefore cannot be said to form the plural by adding **-ra** (which in some nouns triggers a gender shift): **zëra** is nonetheless sometimes (incorrectly) seen followed by a feminine adjective.

　　iii.　First Declension (**-ni** extension):

hu	see dictionary	**hu**

dry	*padlock*	**dryna**

iv. Second Declension:

arkitra	*architrave*	**arkitrarë**
ka	*ox*	**qe**
tra	*beam*	**trarë**
dhe	*earth**	**dhera**
she	*perennial stream*	**shera**
njeri	*man, person*	**njerëz**
shi	*rain*	**shira**

13. Class 13. Nouns ending in **-ua** and other nouns forming plural with **-nj**.

a. This class includes:

i. Most (masculine) nouns ending in **-ua**.

ii. Eight nouns ending in **-n** which change this to **-nj**.

iii. Four nouns ending in **-á** and two in **-ë** forming the plural with **-enj**.

iv. Three nouns ending in **-ër**.

v. A few other First Declension nouns.

vi. All nouns in this Class are stressed on the plural endings.

b. For nouns ending in **-ua** the regular plural ending is **-onj**, as in:

patkua	*horseshoe*	**patkonj**
thua	*fingernail*	**thonj**
vargua	*chain*	**vargonj**

c. Exceptions are:

krua	*spring*	**kroje**
zgjua	*beehive*	**zgjoje**
përrua	*spring, stream*	**përrenj**

d. The following nouns change the final **-n** of the singular stem to **-nj** to form the plural. These nouns are stressed on the final syllable in both singular and plural. Example: **vidan – vidanj**:

bërcan	*big olive*	**vidan**	(male) *pigeon*
carian	*hearthstone*	**bërshen**	*English yew*
gocan	*pumice stone*	**kulmetin**	*water-poplar*
rruvan	*grape stalk*	**barbun**	*red mullet*

e. The following First Declension nouns form the plural with **-enj**:

Group 1	**dhaskal**	*pedant*	**dhaskenj**
	bush	*(mythical) swamp beast*	**bushenj**
Group 3	**lëmë**	*work yard*	**lëmenj**
	lumë	*river*	**lumenj**
Group 4	**budalla**	*fool*	**budallenj**
	fukara	*pauper*	**fukarenj**
	maskara	*scoundrel*	**maskarenj**
	qerrata	*crafty person*	**qerratenj**
Group 6	**përrua**	*stream*	**përrenj**

f. The following nouns form the plural with **-inj,** but in some instances with additions to or other alterations to the stem and in some instances with alternative forms: of those alternative forms only **shkëmbinj** and **shkëmba** differ in meaning:

shkëmb	*cliff*	**shkëmbinj**	**shkëmba**

thelb	*kernel**	thelpinj	
stap	*cudgel*	stapinj	stape
shkop	*stick*	shkopinj	
drapër	*sickle*	drapinj	drapërinj
gjarpër	*snake*	gjarpinj	gjarpërinj
gisht	*finger*	gishtërinj	gishta
prift	*priest*	priftërinj	
zot	*mister*	zotërinj	

g.   i.   **Shkëmb** has a further form **shkëmbenj**.

       ii.   The plural form **shkëmba** has the meaning *chairs, stools*.

h.   **Shpárgër**: *nappy* has plural **shpërgënj**: the stress shifts to the ending in the plural.

14.   <u>Class 14: Nouns forming the plural with -ër</u>:

a.   This Class comprises animate nouns, mostly denoting persons. Some have alternative forms:

bujkrob	*serf*	**bujkrobër**
dom	*Roman Catholic priest*	**domër**
dreq	*devil*	**dreqër**
gjysh	*grandfather*	**gjyshër/ gjysha/ gjyshë**
kec	*goat kid*	**keca /kecër**
mbret	*king*	**mbretër**
nip	*nephew, grandson*	**nipa/ nipër**
princ	*prince*	**princa/ princër**
prind	*parent*	**prindër**
qyq	*person without family*	**qyqër**
rob	*serf**	**robër**
shenjt	*saint*	**shenjtër**
ungj	*uncle* (see Section XXXVI)	**ungjër**

b. Other nouns which form the plural in this way such as **atë, kunat, lugat** and **shtrat** change the stem vowel and are therefore listed under Class 2 d ii.

c. **Vëlla**: *brother* forms plural **vëllezër**.

d. The following form the plural with **-ër** when used figuratively:

Singular	Meaning	Normal Plural	Figurative Plural
buf	*owl*	**bufë**	**bufër**
hajvan	*beast of burden*	**hajvanë**	**hajvanër**
këlysh	*pup*	**këlyshë**	**këlyshër**
qen	*dog*	**qen**	**qenër**
ujk	*wolf*	**ujq**	**ujqër**

15. <u>Class 15: Nouns forming the plural with **-ra**.</u>

a. This Class comprises primarily those masculine substance nouns ending in **-ë** which were formerly neuter together with a small number of other substance nouns. Such nouns are all feminine in the plural, as are **bar** and **mall**, but most other nouns forming the plural with **-ra** remain masculine.

b. The former neuter nouns which have plurals are as follows. In all instances the plural is formed by adding **-ra**, as in **brumë – brumëra, lesh – leshra**:

brumë	*dough*	**miell**	*flour*
djathë	*cheese*	**mish**	*meat*
drithë	*grain*	**mjaltë**	*honey*
dhjamë	*tallow*	**ujë**	*water*
gjalpë	*butter*	**vaj**	*oil*
lesh	*hair, wool*		

c. **Ballë**: *forehead* forms the plural without suffix.

d. The following nouns not ending in -ë also become feminine in the plural: these nouns are listed separately because unlike those at b. above and **ballë** they do not have vestigial neuter forms:

bar	*grass, herb*	**barëra**
mall	*goods*	**mallra**
pleh	*manure*	**plehra**
shi	*rain*	**shira**

e. **Fshatra**, plural of **fshat**: *village*, is sometimes seen with masculine agreement, sometimes feminine.

f. **Barna**: *medicines*, the plural of **bar**, may be feminine.

g. Other nouns which form the plural similarly with the suffix -**ra**, but do not change gender, include:

i. From the First Declension:

bulmet	*dairy product*	**qind**	*hundred*
krem	*cream*	**shpirt**	*spirit, essence*
llum	*sludge, sediment*	**tym**	*smoke*
mut	*excrement* (vulgar)		

ii. From the Second Declension:

byk	*chaff*	**gjak**	*blood*
dhe	*earth, land*	**she**	*perennial stream*

h. The following show minor variations and/or alternative forms:

asht	*bone*	**eshtra**
barut	*gunpowder*	**barutra/barute**

gaz	*gas*	**gazra/gaze**
llosh	*grass, grassy area*	**lloshe/lloshra**
reçel	*jam*	**reçele/ reçelra**
stof	*fabric*	**stofra/stofa**

Lloshra has the meaning of *sweepings, rubbish* or *dandruff*.

i. **Qind**: *hundred* is invariable when used as a cardinal number, but when used as an expression of quantity, without a multiplier, it has the form **qindra**: *hundreds*.

j. **Kundërgaz**: *gasmask* has only one plural form, **kundërgaze**.

k. **Grunjëra**: *wheat crop* or *cereals* (derived from **grurë**: *wheat*) is feminine.

16. Class 16: <u>Nouns forming the plural with the suffixes **-lerë, -llarë**</u>.

a. These nouns are of Turkish origin, and the original plural suffixes of **-llar** and **-ler** have been extended to **-llarë** and **-lerë** by analogy with nouns of Class 5. The suffix is stressed. Except for **baba** and the other relatives, also **hoxhë** and **haxhi**, these nouns are no longer found in modern usage. Among them are:

i. From Group 1 of the First Declension:

| **at** | *saddle horse* | **atllarë** |

ii. From Group 4 of the First Declension:

aga	*landowner*	**agallarë**
baba	*father*	**baballarë**
usta	*master craftsman*	**ustallarë**

        xhaxha   *uncle*   **xhaxhallarë**

iii.   From the Second Declension:

bej (Definite **beu**)	*Feudal landowner*	**bejlerë**
efendi	*respected person*	**efendilerë**
haxhi	*hajji*	**haxhilerë**
kadi	*judge*	**kadilerë**
myfti	*mufti*	**myftilerë/myftinj**
sheh	*Bektashi leader*	**shehlerë**

iv.   From the Third Declension (with suffix **-allarë**):

axhë	*uncle*	**axhallarë**
dajë	*uncle*	**dajallarë**
hoxhë	*holy person*	**hoxhallarë**

b.   **Dajë** and **axhë** have alternative plurals **axhë** and **daja**.

17.   <u>Class 17: Nouns with alternative plurals</u>.

a.   This Class can be divided into:

i.   Homonyms.

ii.   Nouns which have alternative plural forms to distinguish different shades of a (broad) singular meaning.

iii.   Nouns which have alternative plural forms which do not convey different meanings.

b.   Many nouns of all three categories have been covered already, and those from category iii. will not be re-listed.

c. Homonyms covered in other Noun Classes are as follows:

Class 1	**as**	Class 6	**gaz**
Class 1	**tas**	Class 6	**bel**
Class 1/12	**hu**	Class 6	**element**
Class 2	**asht**	Class 7	**fil**
Class 3	**çek**	Class 8	**kampion**
Class 3	**gjak**	Class 8	**milion**
Class 4	**llosh**	Class 9	**çam**
Class 5	**bar**	Class 12	**bli**
Class 5	**ton**	Class 13	**shkëmb**

d. Homonyms with other endings are as follows:

i. **Milion**: *million* and **miliard**: *milliard* (one thousand million) both form the plural with -ë when used as numbers, but with -a when used to express quantities. Thus:

I KEK-ut janë alokuar 20 milionë euro: *20 million euros have been allocated to the Kosova Energy Corporation* (**Koha ditore**): and

Miliona euro janë shpenzuar në rindërtimin e infrastrukturës: *millions of euros were spent in rebuilding the infrastructure.*

ii. **Rreth**: *circle/circular object* has plural **rrathë**.

Rreth: *administrative area* has plural **rrethe**.

iii. **Vaj**: *oil* forms plural **vajra** while **vaj**: *dirge* forms plural **vaje**.

iv. **Balç**: *balsam flower* forms plural **balça**, whereas **balç**: *shoelace* forms plural **balçe**.

e. The following nouns have different plural forms to convey different aspects of the singular meaning:

i. **Vit** has alternative plural forms **vite** and **vjet**. After numbers and expressions of quantity **vjet** is used, while **vite** is used in other instances. Examples are:

Pesë vjet: *five years*, **vitet e shkollës**: *schooldays*.

ii. **Zot** has alternative plural forms depending on its meaning; **zota**; *gods* and **zotërinj**: *gentlemen* (used as a form of address).

iii. **Frut/fryt** has alternative plurals depending on whether it is used in its basic meaning or its figurative meaning: **frytet e punës**: *the fruits of work* and **fruta e perime**: *fruit and vegetables*.

iv. Nouns with alternative plurals with figurative meanings ending in **-ër** have been covered in Class 14.

f. The following nouns do not belong to any ending-based Class but have alternative plurals, mostly in **-a** and **-e**, but without variation in meaning:

bisht	*tail*	**bishta**	**bishtra**
çap	*step*	**çapa**	**çape**
djep	*cradle*	**djepa**	**djepe**
efektiv	*personnel*	**efektiva**	**efektive**
gjedh	*neat, cattle*	**gjedhë**	**gjedhe**

g. **Flamur**: *flag* has alternative forms, depending on the stress used. The plural of **flámur** is **flámuj** whereas the plural of **flamúr** is **flamurë**.

18. <u>Irregular plural formations</u>.

a. The following do not follow any of the patterns set out previously:

djalë	*boy, son*	**djem**
djalosh	*lad*	**djelmosha**
dhëndër	*bridegroom, son-in-law*	**dhëndurë**
gëthep	See dictionary	**gëthapë**
ipeshkëv	*Roman Catholic bishop*	**ipeshkvij**
ka	*ox*	**qe**
kalë	*horse*	**kuaj**
kinoteatër	*cinema/ theatre*	**kinoteatro**
krye	*head*	**krerë**
kuadër	*team*	**kuadro**
malazias	*Montenegrin*	**malazez**
njeri	*person*	**njerëz**
teatër	*theatre*	**teatro/ teatra**
thes	*sack*	**thasë**
vëlla	*brother*	**vëllezër**

b. The plural form **dhëndurë** has the stress on the **u**.

c. The Definite forms of these nouns are as shown:

djalë	**djali**	**djemtë**
djalosh	**djaloshi**	**djelmoshat**
dhëndër	**dhëndri**	**dhëndurët**
gëthep	**gëthepi**	**gëthapët**
ipeshkëv	**ipeshkvi**	**ipeshkvijtë**
ka	**kau**	**qetë**
kalë	**kali**	**kuajt**
kinoteatër	**kinoteatri**	**kinoteatrot**
krye	**kreu**	**krerët**
kuadër	**kuadri**	**kuadrot**
malazias	**malaziasi**	**malazezit**
njeri	**njeriu**	**njerëzit**

teatër	teatri	teatrot/ teatrat
thes	thesi	thasët
vëlla	vëllai	vëllezërit

d. In **Gramatikë historike e gjuhës shqipe** some irregular forms no longer in general use are listed:

Singular	Meaning	Regular Pl.	Irregular Pl.
kalli	*ear of wheat*	**kallinj**	**kallëz**.
plëndës	*stomach*	**plëndësa**	**plëndásë**
thek	*tassel*	**thekë**	**thakë**

19. <u>Suppletive Plurals.</u>

a. A few masculine nouns denoting livestock have suppletive plurals (i.e. plurals formed from a different stem), but these are no longer in current use. They were listed in the 1954 edition of **Fj. Sh.s.**, namely:

Noun	Meaning	Old Plural	Modern Plural
edh	*goat-kid*	**dhiz**	**edha**
qengj	*lamb*	**shtjerra**	**qengja**
viç	*calf*	**vjeta**	**viça**

b. The one suppletive of this type which is in current use is feminine, namely **dhen**, plural of **dele**: *ewe*. However **shtjerra** is related to **shqerra** (see III 13 b).

20. <u>Neuter nouns.</u>

a. Most neuter nouns become feminine in the plural.

b. Of neuter nouns which have become more or less masculine, **ballë** belongs to Class 1, while the remainder (substance nouns) are covered in Class 15.

c. **Krye**: *head* forms plural **krerë**.

XVI   PLURAL DECLENSION: FEMININE NOUNS

Note: Throughout this Section references to the stem are to the Plural Indefinite stem.

1. As explained previously, feminine nouns decline in the plural in exactly the same way as masculine nouns with similar plural endings, with the exception of FPG 4, which consists of two irregular plurals. Nonetheless the Declension Groups are set out here again. The Group numbers correspond to those of the Masculine Plural Groups; there is however no FPG 6.

2. FPG 1

   Nouns with stem ending in -ë:

	Indefinite	Definite
Nominative	ditë	ditët
Accusative	ditë	ditët
Genitive	i/e ditëve	i/e ditëve
Dative	ditëve	ditëve
Ablative	ditësh/ ditëve	ditëve

3. FPG 2

   Nouns with unstressed vowel ending:

	Indefinite	Definite
Nominative	vajza	vajzat
Accusative	vajza	vajzat
Genitive	i/e vajzave	i/e vajzave
Dative	vajzave	vajzave
Ablative	vajzash/ vazjave	vajzave

4. FPG 3

   Nouns with stem ending in a stressed vowel:

	Indefinite	Definite
Nominative	**shtëpi**	**shtëpitë**
Accusative	**shtëpi**	**shtëpitë**
Genitive	**i/e shtëpive**	**i/e shtëpive**
Dative	**shtëpive**	**shtëpive**
Ablative	**shtëpish/ shtëpive**	**shtëpive**

5. FPG 4

   Nouns ending in -**l**, -**r**, -**s** and -**z**:

	Indefinite	Definite
Nominative	**duar**	**duart**
Accusative	**duar**	**duart**
Genitive	**i/e duarve**	**i/e duarve**
Dative	**duarve**	**duarve**
Ablative	**duarsh/ duarve**	**duarve**

   Dyer (plural of **derë**) declines similarly.

6. FPG 5

   Nouns with stem ending in a single consonant other than -**j**, -**l**, -**r**, -**s**, -**t** and -**z**:

	Indefinite	Definite
Nominative	**dhen**	**dhentë**
Accusative	**dhen**	**dhentë**
Genitive	**i/e dhenve**	**i/e dhenve**
Dative	**dhenve**	**dhenve**
Ablative	**dhensh/ dhenve**	**dhenve**

   Drunj declines similarly.

7. FPG 7: Noun ending in -t: **net** (plural of **natë**):

	Indefinite	Definite
Nominative	**net**	**netët**
Accusative	**net**	**netët**
Genitive	**i/e netëve**	**i/e netëve**
Dative	**netëve**	**netëve**
Ablative	**netësh/ netëve**	**netëve**

8. FPG 8: Substantivised Adjectives:

a. With **a** stem

	Indefinite	Definite
Nominative	**të reja**	**të rejat**
Accusative	**të reja**	**të rejat**
Genitive	**i/e të rejave**	**i/e të rejave**
Dative	**të rejave**	**të rejave**
Ablative	**të rejash/ të rejave**	**të rejave**

b. With **e** stem

	Indefinite	Definite
Nominative	**të pashme**	**të pashmet**
Accusative	**të pashme**	**të pashmet**
Genitive	**i/e të pashmeve**	**i/e të pashmeve**
Dative	**të pashmeve**	**të pashmeve**
Ablative	**të pashmesh/të pashmeve**	**të pashmeve**

c. Formed from Participle

	Indefinite	Definite
Nominative	**të ditura**	**të diturat**
Accusative	**të ditura**	**të diturat**
Genitive	**i/e të diturave**	**i/e të diturave**
Dative	**të diturave**	**të diturave**
Ablative	**të diturash/të diturave**	**të diturave**

XVII PLURAL FORMATION CLASSES: FEMININE NOUNS

1. By comparison with masculine nouns, the formation of the plural of feminine nouns is relatively straightforward. One reason is that the range of endings is much smaller. Feminine nouns fall into two main groups: those which retain the same form in the (Indefinite) Nominative and Accusative plural as in the singular, and those which add -**a**.

2. The major difficulty is in determining which nouns ending in -**ë** remain unaltered in the plural, i.e. restoring the -**ë** and which add -**a** or -**ra** in place of the -**ë** of the CF. The overwhelming majority forms the plural with -**a**, particularly animate nouns. There is no straightforward way of determining which ending is used: however all derived nouns form plural with -**a**, while substance nouns mostly form the plural with -(**ë**) **ra**.

3. The classes based on plural formation have been numbered to correspond with the masculine Classes.

4. Classes 10F and 11F include neuter nouns formed from gerunds, which become feminine in the plural.

4. Class 1F: Nouns with identical singular and plural forms.

a. This group comprises:

i. Nouns ending in a stressed vowel, including monosyllabics, except **dru**, **gjë**, **rixha**, **pëlle**, **zotëri**, **e re** and **e ve**, thus effectively subsuming Class 12F.

ii. Nouns ending in unstressed -**e** and -**o**.

iii. 5 animate nouns and 101 inanimate nouns with CF ending in -**ë**, of which some have literary plurals, as detailed below, and some have two plural forms which differ in meaning. Most nouns with CF ending in -**ë** form plural with -**a**.

b.i. Examples of nouns with stressed vowel ending are:

kala	*castle**	**dhi**	*nanny-goat*
para	*money*	**taksi**	*taxi*
re	*cloud**	**byro**	*office*

ii. The following have alternative plurals ending in -**ra**:

Singular	Meaning	Normal plural	Alternative
bela	*nuisance*	**bela**	**belara**
shaka	*joke*	**shaka**	**shakara**
magji	*magic*	**magji**	**magjira**

iii. Some nouns in this group have alternative plurals used for literary purposes to convey certain nuances, as in:

Liza në botën e çudirave: *Alice in Wonderland.*

These should not be used in everyday speech or writing.

	Singular	Meaning	Normal plural	Literary plural
	kala	*castle*	**kala**	**kalara**
	ide	*idea*	**ide**	**idera**
	çudi	*surprise*	**çudi**	**çudira**
	gosti	*banquet*	**gosti**	**gostira**
	hordhi	*horde*	**hordhi**	**hordhira**
	kusi	*flat-bottomed pot*	**kusi**	**kusira**
	marrëzi	*absurdity*	**marrëzi**	**marrëzira**
	mrekulli	*miracle*	**mrekulli**	**mrekullira**
	stoli	*decoration*	**stoli**	**stolira**
	tepsi	*baking-sheet*	**tepsi**	**tepsira**
	trimëri	*act of bravery*	**trimëri**	**trimërira**

iv. The archaic word **rixhá**: *request* has plural **rixhára**.

v. **Kashaí**: *currycomb* and **okllaí**: *rolling pin* belong to this Class. So does **rubaí**: (a type of Oriental verse form, as in "The Rubaiyat of Omar Khayyam"); however the translation by Fan Noli bears the title **Rubairat e të famshmit Omar Khajam**.

vi. **Pëlle**: *milch cow* (or other milking animal) forms plural **pëlla**, and **gjë**: *thing* has plural **gjëra**.

c.i. The nouns ending in unstressed -e include the large number of deverbal nouns ending in -ie/je (although many of these do not have plurals), and those feminine nouns such as **mjeke**: *female doctor* which are derived from masculine nouns.

ii. Examples of endings in unstressed -e or -o are:

	arsyje	*reason*	**arsyje**
	anije	*boat*	**anije**
	depo	*depot*	**depo**

iii. **Bóa**: *boa constrictor* has one form, **boa** for both Definite and Indefinite Nominative singular.

iv. **Huá**: *loan* belongs to this Class, but **grua**: *woman* forms plural **gra**.

v. **Dele**: *ewe* has a regular plural **dele** and an alternative suppletive plural **dhen**, as mentioned at Section XV, Paragraph 19.

d. Nouns ending in -**ë**: The overwhelming majority forms the plural with -**a**, including most animate nouns. Because of their large number (106 listed in **Fjalori i gjuhës shqipe së sotme**, nouns forming the plural with -**ë** (Class 1F) are listed in Section F.

i. Some nouns in this Class have compounds which form the plural with -**a**. These include:

hekurudhë	*railway*	**hekurudha**
lulëkëmborë	*bluebell*	**lulëkëmbora**
mushmollë	*medlar*	**mushmolla**

ii. **Gradë** has various homonyms: some of these have an alternative plural **grada**: **Fjalori i gjuhës shqipe së sotme** covers these.

iii. Those nouns listed in Part F and marked ♥ have homonyms with plurals ending in -**a**:

Homonym	Meaning of homonym	Plural of homonym
algë	*seaweed*	**alga**
rrënjë	*live-oak*	**rrënja**
shalë	*saddle*	**shala**
urë	*bridge*	**ura**

iv. The following nouns listed in Part F and marked ♣ have alternative plurals ending in -**a** and -**ë** without any apparent difference in meaning:

    dardhë   *pear*
    klasë   *class*

e. Of the other nouns ending in -**ë**:

i. **Copë**: *piece*, **gjuhë**: *tongue* or *language* and **kohë**: *time* have alternative literary forms as listed at v. below.

ii. **Bukë**: *bread* has alternative plural forms **bukë**: *loaves* and **bukëra**: *crumbs*.

iii. Some nouns ending in -**ë** have different forms of the plural indicating alternative meanings. These are listed under Class 17F below.

iv. **Okë** is an old unit of measurement approximately equivalent to 2.8 lbs. (1.24 Kg.), but has numerous idiomatic uses.

v. Some nouns in this group have alternative plurals used for literary purposes to convey certain nuances. These forms should not be used in everyday speech or writing. These include:

copë	*piece*	**copë**	**copëra**
gjuhë	*tongue/language*	**gjuhë**	**gjuhëra**
kohë	*time*	**kohë**	**kohëra**

vi. The following feminine nouns ending in -**ë**, being irregular are listed under Paragraph 11 of this Section:

derë, dorë, dizgë, kallcë, natë.

5. **Class 2F. Nouns changing the stem vowel..**

The few feminine nouns which change the stem vowel to form the plural are irregular and therefore listed under Paragraph 11.

6. **Class 8F. Nouns forming the plural with -e.**

This Class comprises those masculine nouns which form the plural with **-e** and thus become feminine. No feminine noun uses the suffix **-e**.

7. **Class 10F: Nouns ending in -ël, -ën, -ër, -ërr, -ëz, -uar, -ul, -ull and -ur forming plural with -a.**

a. This Class comprises nouns forming the plural with **-a**, with endings in **-ël, -ën, -ër, -ërr, -ëz, -uar, -ul, -ull** and **-ur**. The nouns ending in **-ëz** and **-uar** are too numerous to list, but for the others see the lists in Part F.

b. Feminine nouns ending in a consonant, viz. **-ël, -ën, -ër, -ërr, -ëz -uar, -ul, -ull** and **-ur** all form the plural in **-a**, but the **ë** of the CF is dropped before **-ël, -ën, -ër** and **-ërr**. Examples are:

vegël	*instrument*	**vegla**
lisën	*thyme*	**lisna**
femër	*woman*	**femra**
fshikëz	*bladder*	**fshikëza**
fabul	*fable*	**fabula**
kumbull	*plum*	**kumbulla**
flutur	*butterfly*	**flutura**

See Part F for a fuller listing. A few nouns with these endings do not have plural forms.

c. **Vjehërr**: *mother-in-law* forms plural **vjehrra**.

d. Other feminine nouns ending in a consonant as listed in Part F also take **-a** as the plural ending.

e. Those gerunds which can form a plural such as **të bërtitur**: *shouting* become feminine in the plural and take the suffix **-a**.

f. Feminine gerunds such as **e shtuar**: *addition* form the plural with **a**.

8. <u>Class 11F. Nouns ending in -ë</u>.

a. This Class comprises the overwhelming majority of feminine nouns ending in -ë, apart from those from Class 1F listed in Section F, and those comprised in Classes 15F and 17F. It includes gerunds ending in **-në** and **-rë**, which become feminine in the plural.

b. The standard plural ending is **-a**, in place of the final -ë of the CF.

c. Most animate nouns in -ë belong to this Class, the main exceptions being **bletë**, **kafshë**, **kumbarë**, **lopë** and **shtazë**.

d. All derived nouns such as **ftesë**: *invitation* and **dëftesë**: *receipt* belong to this Class.

e. Examples include:

barkë	*boat*	**barka**
dhuratë	*gift*	**dhurata**
hekurudhë	*railway*	**hekurudha**
lopatë	*spade*	**lopata**
nënë	*mother*	**nëna**

f. The following nouns which form the plural in -a have homonyms ending in -ë, as listed at 4 c ii above:

algë *seaweed* **shalë** *saddle*
rrënjë *live-oak* **urë** *bridge*

g. **Verë**: *summer* forms plural **vera**, while its homonym **verë**: *wine* forms plural **verëra**.

h. **Erë**: *era* has plural **era**, while its homonym **erë**: *wind, smell* has plural **erëra**.

9. Class 12F: Nouns with stressed vowel stem.

This Class has two nouns: **dru**: *firewood*, which forms plural **dru** or **drunj**, and the archaic word **rixha**: *request*, which has plural **rixhara**. **Zotëri**: *master*, which forms plural **zotërinj**, is masculine and listed in Class 12. All other feminine nouns ending in a stressed vowel, except for **pëlle**: *milch cow* (irregular) have identical singular and plural forms and therefore belong in Class 1F. **E re**: *young woman* and **e ve**: *widow*, as substantivised adjectives, form the plural with the clitic **të** and the ending **-ja**.

10. Class 15F: Nouns forming the plural with -ra.

a. This Class contains:

i. Nouns ending in -ë mostly denoting substances.

ii. **Meze** (when stressed on the second syllable), **rixha** (see Class 12 F) and **tagji**.

iii. **Dhjetë** and **mijë**: when used not as numbers but as expressions of quantity: see Part D (NUMBERS).

iv.   **Filozofi** (see below).

b.   Substance and similar nouns ending in -**ë** as listed below. The plural formation is analogous to those masculine substance nouns of Class 15 which become feminine in the plural. The most commonly found are:

baltë	*mud**	**baltëra/balta**
bojë	*colour*	**bojëra**
borë	*snow*	**borëra**
cohë	*fabric, serge**	**cohëra**
erë	*wind*	**erëra**
farë	*seed*	**farëra/fara**
gjë	*thing*	**gjëra**
kashtë	*straw*	**kashtëra**
kripë	*salt*	**kripëra**
lojë	*game*	**lojëra/lojna**
luftë	*war, conflict*	**luftëra**
verë	*wine*	**verëra**

c.   Do not confuse **erë**: *wind* with **erë**: *era*, which has plural **era**, and **verë**: *wine* with **verë**: *summer* which has plural **vera**.

d.   **Copë** has three plural forms, including **copëra**. See Class 17F.

e.   **Meze**: *appetizer* may be stressed on either syllable; when stressed on the second syllable it has alternative plural **mezera**.

f.   **Filozofi**: *philosophy* has plural form **filozofira** used in a derogatory sense to mean *wild ideas*.

g.   **Tagji**: *horse feed* forms plural **tagjira**

h.   For the plurals of **akrobaci**: *acrobatics* see Class 17F.

i. **Jetëra**: *lives* and **gjellëra**: *dishes*, formed by analogy with the above, are sometimes seen but are not accepted as Standard Albanian.

11. Class 17F: Nouns with alternative plural forms.

a. The following nouns have alternative plural forms depending on the meaning of the plural word:

brinjë	**brinjë**	**brinja**
bukë	**bukë**	**bukëra**
copë	**copë**	**copa/copëra**
grykë	**grykë**	**gryka**
kokë	**kokë**	**koka**
lëkurë	**lëkurë**	**lëkura**
palë	**palë**	**pala**
petë	**petë**	**(peta)**
pikë	**pikë**	**pika**
rrënjë	**rrënjë**	**rrënja**
urë	**urë**	**ura**

b. The different meanings are:

i. **Brinjë** : *ribs* (anatomical): **Brinja**: *flanks, edges*.

ii. **Bukë**: *loaves*: **Bukëra**: *crumbs*.

iii. **Copë**: used to express quantity, as in **një mijë copë tulla**: *one thousand bricks* (cf. German *Stück*):

Copa: fragments, as in **tri copa letre**: *three pieces (fragments) of paper*. The alternative plural **copëra** has the same meaning.

iv. **Grykë**: *throats*, also various illnesses as **Grykët e bardha**: *diphtheria*:

        Gryka: *gorges* (topographical) or *muzzles* (of guns.)

v.   **Kokë**: *head* (as in *head of cattle*):

        Koka: *head* (anatomical and figurative).

vi.   **Lëkurë**: *hides*, i.e. *skins removed from animals*:

        Lëkura: *skins*, i.e. *outer covering of fruit, vegetable, human or animal*.

vii. **Palë**: *pair, set, side* (as in **dy palë pantallona**: *two pairs of trousers* and **të dyja palët**: *both sides*):

        Pala: *dried figs* or *pile of cured tobacco leaves*.

viii. **Petë**: *layers*, as in **petët e byrekut**: *layers of pastry in a burek*:

        Peta as such is not used, but the Ablative Plural occurs in **lloj petash**: *game played with small flat stones*.

ix. **Pikë**: *points* (as in a game):

        Pika: *drops* (e.g. *raindrops*), *spots*.

c.   **Mijë**: *thousand* has the form **mijë** when used as a cardinal number, but **mijëra** when used to mean *thousands*. **Dhjetë**: *ten* has a corresponding form **dhjetëra**, literally *tens* but in practice more fluently translated as *scores*. See Part D for details of usage.

d.   **Akrobaci**: *acrobatics* (regular plural **akrobaci**) has an alternative form **akrobacira** meaning *sharp practice*.

12. The following are irregular:

derë	*door*	**dyer**
e diel	*Sunday*	**të diela**
dizgë	(*cradle*) *band*	**dizgje**
dorë	*hand*	**duar**
grua	*woman*	**gra**
kallcë	*legging* ø*	**kallca/ kallçina**
natë	*night*	**net**
pëlle	*milch cow**	**pëlla**

13. Substantivised adjectives do not alter their declension forms; thus **e re**: *young girl*, forms plural **të reja** and **e ve**: *widow* forms plural **të veja**.

14. **Gramatika historike e gjuhës shqipe** cites some obsolete irregular plurals: **të ra** and **të va** from **e re** and **e ve** respectively, while for **rre**: *footpath* (normal plural **rre**) the alternative **rra** is shown.

XVIII ARTICULATED NOUNS

1. The use of the clitic before **atë** and **ëmë** and other close relatives with the meaning *his/her/their* is discussed in Section XX.

2. Substantivised adjectives are also preceded by Clitics, the form of the Clitic being as shown in the (Noun) Declension Tables.

3. Neuter nouns are all articulated, except for **ballë** and **krye** and the substance nouns listed at VII 7 above.

4. As neuter nouns, Gerunds, which are formed from participles, are articulated. They are also articulated

when they are declined as feminine nouns, as in **e shtuar**: *supplement*, **e ngrënë**: *eating*.

5. Some articulated nouns exist in their own right, i.e. are not derived from an adjective. Examples are:

   E folme: *dialect, regional idiom,* **e diel**: *Sunday*.

XIX SUBSTANTIVISED ADJECTIVES

1. As in other languages, Albanian adjectives can be used as nouns, in both genders. When so used they are invariably preceded by a Clitic, the form of which is set out in the Noun Declension Tables.

2. Such nouns have both Definite and Indefinite Forms, as in **një i huaj**: *a foreigner*, **i huaji**: *the foreigner*.

3. An adjective can be qualified by an adverb before becoming substantivised, e.g. **i sapoarrituri**: *the person who has just arrived*.

4. An adjective in the comparative degree may be used as a noun, in the Indefinite Form:

   Ma jepni një më të vogël: *give me a smaller one*.

5. An adjective in the superlative degree may be used as a noun, in the Definite Form:

   Ky është më i shtrejnti: *this is the most expensive one*.

6. **E ve**: *widow* forms plural **e veja**. **I ve**: *widower* (plural **të ve**) belongs to the Second Declension.

XX NOUNS WITH PREPOSED POSSESSIVE ADJECTIVES

1. A small group of nouns, mostly denoting members of the family, can be found with the possessive adjective placed before the noun. The group includes:

	Masculine		Feminine
atë	*father*	**ëmë**	*mother*
bir	*son*	**bijë**	*daughter*
baba	*father*	**nënë**	*mother*
vëlla	*brother*	**motër**	*sister*
nip	*nephew/ grandson*	**mbesë**	*niece/ granddaughter*
gjysh	*grand-father*	**gjyshe**	*grandmother*
kushëri	*cousin*	**kushërirë**	*cousin*
kunat	*brother-in-law*	**kunatë**	*sister-in-law*
ungj	*uncle*	**emtë**	*aunt*
vjehërr	*father-in-law*	**vjehërr**	*mother-in-law*
shoq	*husband*	**shoqe**	*wife*
njerk	*stepfather*	**njerkë**	*stepmother*
zot	*lord*	**zonjë**	*mistress*

2. The declension of **atë** (or **at**) and **ëmë** differs depending on the preceding possessive. After **im/ime yt/jot ynë/jon** and **juaj** the Indefinite Form is used, whereas after **i** and **e**, which in this context mean *his, her, their*, a Definite Form is used. There is a further Definite Form for use without a preceding possessive. In this usage the possessives have special forms.

	First Person	Second Person	Third Person	Definite
Nominative	im atë	yt atë	i ati	ati
Accusative	tim atë	tët atë	t'anë	atin
Genitive	i/e tim eti	i/e tyt eti	i/e t'et	i/e etit
Dative/Abl.	tim eti	tyt eti	t'et	etit

Tyt and **tët** are interchangeable. It can be seen that the feminine forms of the possessive, including **jone**, which is not shown, in this usage lack the final **e**.

	First Person	Second Person	Third Person
Nominative	**ime ëmë**	**jot ëmë**	**e ëma**
Accusative	**time ëmë**	**tët ëmë**	**t'ëmën**
Genitive	**i/e sime ëme**	**i/e sat ëma**	**i/e s'ëmës**
Dative/Abl.	**sime ëme**	**sat ëma**	**s'ëmës**

3. **Emë** has plural **ëma** and declines normally; the plural declension of **atë** is as follows:

	Indefinite	Definite
Nominative	**etër**	**etërit**
Accusative	**etër**	**etërit**
Genitive	**i/e etërve**	**i/e etërve**
Dative	**etërve**	**etërve**
Ablative	**etërish**	**etërve**

4. The possessives shown above can also be used with other nouns denoting close kinship, such as **vëlla** and **motër**. When used before nouns beginning with a consonant, **të** and **së** are written in full.

5. The third person possessive used with plural nouns such as **vëllezërit** and **motrat** is in all cases **të**.

6. If the Clitic **së**, when used with the Genitive case of an articulated noun as in **së motrës**, is preceded by a Feminine Noun in an Oblique case of the Definite Form, then the **së** Clitic which would normally follow that noun is replaced by **të**, as in :

Para shtëpisë të së motrës: *in front of his sister's house.*

XXI **COMPOUND NOUNS**

1. Albanian nouns can be formed by compounding two words, one of which is usually a noun.

2. Commonly deverbal nouns are compounded with other nouns:

a. Agent-nouns, such as **zëdhënës**: *spokesman*.

b. Gerundial nouns, such as **kokëçarje**: *problem*.

3. Two nouns of related meaning can combine, such as **thashetheme**: *gossip, rumour* and **shitblerje**: *commerce*.

4. Adverbs can also combine with nouns as in **bashkatdhetar**: *compatriot*, **keqardhje**: *regret*, **mirëmbajtje**: *maintenance*.

5. Occasionally adjectives combine with nouns, but the result is more commonly an adjective.

6. Compounds normally decline according to the final element, the exceptions being units of measurement such as **kale-fuqi**: *horsepower*, most compounds with **peshk**: *fish* as their first element, and **shtëpi-muze**: *house dedicated as a museum* and **qytet-muze**: *museum town*.

7. Certain compound nouns form the plural differently from their final component. Among these are:

a. Masculine:

Compound	Meaning	Plural	Source plural
deledash	*hermaphrodite*	**deledashë**	**desh**

fishekzjarr	*firework*	**fishekzjarrë**	*zjarre*
hidrokarbur	*hydrocarbon*	**hidrokarbure**	*karburë*
kilovat	*kilowatt*	**kilovatë**	*vat*
kilovolt	*kilovolt*	**kilovoltë**	*volt*
kinoteatër	*cinema and theatre*	**kinoteatro**	*teatra/ teatro*
kryemyfti	*chief mufti*	**kryemyftinj**	*myftinj/ myftilerë*
kundërgaz	*gas mask*	**kundërgaze**	*gaze/gazra*
peshkaqen	*dogfish*	**peshkaqenë**	*qen*
qymyrgur	*coal*	**qymyrgure**	*gurë*

b. Feminine:

Compound	Meaning	Plural	Source plural
hekurudhë	*railway*	**hekurudha**	**udhë**
lulëkëmborë	*bluebell*	**lulëkëmbora**	**këmborë**
mushmollë	*medlar*	**mushmolla**	**mollë**

8. Inconsistencies arise with compounds based on:

a. **Fon** and **plan**: see notes in Section XV, Paragraph 5.

b. **Çikël**: see notes in Section XV, Paragraph 10.

9. Compounds based on **gram** fall into two groups. Units of weight form the plural with **ë** while words using the Greek root *gram* form plurals with **e**.

XXII **ACRONYMS AND ABBREVIATIONS**

1. Nouns formed by abbreviation can be either portmanteau words **(shkurtesat e tipit rrokjesor)** composed of syllables of two or more words, such as **agjitprop**: *agitation and propaganda*, or abbreviations **(shkurtesat e tipit nistor-shkronjor)**

where the initial letters of the component word do not make a pronounceable word) or acronyms (**shkurtesat e tipit nistor-tingullor**), which can be pronounced.

2. <u>Portmanteau words</u> take their gender and declension from the last syllable of the word.

3. <u>Abbreviations and acronyms</u> do not take their gender from the gender of the principal component, but in accordance with the rules below. Such nouns are almost invariably used in the Definite Form: the ending will be separated from the word by a hyphen, and written in lower case. The few plurals take the form of the last element, as in **VIP-a**: *VIP's*.

4. <u>Abbreviations</u>: the letters cannot be pronounced as a word, and the component letters are therefore pronounced as individual letters, e.g. **OKB-ja** (**Organizata e Kombeve të Bashkuara**: *United Nations*), **PSSP-ja** (**Përfaqësues Special i Sekretarit të Përgjithshëm**: *Special Representative of the* (United Nations) *Secretary-General*) Such nouns are invariably feminine: however, because the Special Representative is a person, readers should not be surprised to see the incorrect form **PSSP-i**.

5. <u>Acronyms</u>: the gender depends on the final letter. Those ending in a consonant are masculine (First or Second Declension), such as **MEF-I**, **KEK-u** and **OPEK-u**, whereas those ending in a vowel are feminine, such as **NATO-ja**. Feminine acronyms and abbreviations follow Group 6 of the Third Declension.

6. Mixed acronyms are feminine if the last part is **shkronjor**: *spelt*, as **BEKD-ja**, but masculine regardless of the final letter if the last part is **tingullor**: *pronounced*, as in **NTUS-i** and **BKPOR-i**.

XXIII NOUNS USED IN PHRASAL VERBS

1. Albanian, like English, has a large number of phrasal verbs. A noun forming part of a phrasal verb will be in the Indefinite Accusative, and there will be no Object Clitic before the verb.

2. The meaning of such phrasal verbs may sometimes be close to the meaning of the component parts, at other times less close. Consider the following examples:

   vë re, jap fund, marr vesh, heq dorë.

3. Phrasal verbs can be used impersonally, e.g.:

   kihet parasysh.

XXIV GENDER SHIFT IN NOUNS

1. The most widespread example of Gender Shift in Albanian is provided by those masculine nouns which form the plural by adding the suffix **-e**. These nouns are all inanimate (except for a very few) and mostly abstract, and include all deverbal nouns ending in **-im**.

2. Masculine nouns which form the plural with the suffix **-ra** are likewise mostly feminine in the plural. Again these are inanimate, generally refer to substances, and many were originally neuter. See Section XV, Class 15 for more details. This change of gender occurs only where **-ra** is a suffix and does not affect all nouns which have **-ra** as the last two letters of the plural, e.g. **emra** and **libra**. The ending is **-a** and so they remain masculine. Examples of nouns which change gender, and require feminine agreement, include:

djathëra: *(types of) cheese* **ujëra**: *(quantity of) water*.

3. **Fshatra**: *villages* is used with both masculine and feminine agreement.

4. **Zëra**: *voices* and **teatro**: *theatres* are sometimes (incorrectly) seen with feminine agreement.

5. When used in the plural Gerunds become feminine.

6. The following animate nouns which form the plural by the suffix **-e** thereby become feminine:

Class	Noun	Meaning	Plural
3	**beng**	*Golden Oriole*	**bengje**
	molusk	*mollusc*	**molusqe**
3	**stërhell**	*tall thin person*	**stërheje**
	shtërg	*stork*	**shtërgje**
5	**kurban**	*sacrificial animal*	**kurbane**
	bakter	*bacterium*	**baktere**
6	**kalëdet**	*seahorse*	**kalëdete**
	personalitet	*personality*	**personalitete**
7	**bacil**	*bacillus*	**bacile**
8	**insekt**	*insect*	**insekte**
	mikrob	*microbe*	**mikrobe**
	personazh	*personage*	**personazhe**
	virus	*virus*	**viruse**

7. Since masculine Third Declension nouns such as **qole**: *servile person* and **qose**: *beardless person* do not add a suffix to form the plural, they remain masculine.

8. Some sources cite the plurals **hapa**: *steps* and **kolektiva**: *collective farms* as having feminine gender.

9. **Rresht**: *row* and **petk**: *cloak* (both formerly neuter) form plurals with **-a**, becoming feminine in the plural.

10. The effect of gender shift, requiring feminine agreement, can be seen in these examples:

Dëshmitë e nxjerra nga këto burime të dorës së parë: *evidence from these primary sources* (**T.Gj.rr.**)

Prapa mureve të larta: *behind high walls* (Teodor Laço, **Vdekja e nëpunësit X**)

Asnjëra nga dyqane private në Prishtinë: *none of the private shops in Prishtina* (**Koha ditore**).

XXV <u>STRESS IN NOUNS</u>

1. There is no fixed stress pattern in Albanian. However these principles may be deduced as to stress in nouns:

a. Monosyllabics are by definition treated as being stressed on the final syllable.

b. Prefixes are not normally stressed.

c. The stress normally remains on the same syllable throughout all declined forms in the singular.

d. The stress normally remains on the same syllable throughout all declined forms in the plural.

e. The stress remains on the same syllable in both singular and plural forms, except as set out below.

2. In the following instances stress shifts in declension:

a. Nouns forming the plural by adding vowel + **-nj**, such as **lumë - luménj, shkop - shkopínj**. (Most nouns forming the plural with **-nj** end in a stressed vowel, and so it is only those which add a syllable as above which suffer stress change).

b. Nouns forming the plural with the suffixes **-llarë** and **-lerë**, where the stress shifts to the suffix.

c. **Dhëndër**, which has plural **dhëndúrë**.

d. **Njeri** as a Second Declension Noun is stressed on the final vowel, but in the plural **njerëz** the first syllable is stressed.

e. **Krye, gavyell** and **pëlqyer**, all of which shed the **y-** of the diphthong within the singular declension as well as throughout the plural, move the stress from the penultimate syllable in the CF to the last syllable of the stem in other forms.

f. **Shpargër**: *nappy shifts* the stress to the ending in the plural **shpërgënj**.

3. Except as above inflectional suffixes are not stressed.

4. The result of 3. above is that although a syllable containing -**ë**- is normally unstressed, where **ë** is the stem vowel, as in **zëri** or **shullëre**, the stress will fall on the **ë** and not on the inflectional suffix.

5. Many formational suffixes (as opposed to inflectional suffixes), such as **-ar, -or** and **-tor** are stressed. If this were not so Group 4 nouns (for example) could not have the plural ending -**ë**, since in modern Albanian a final -**ë** can only follow a stressed syllable.

6. The endings **-all, -ell, -ill** and **-oll** are all stressed, but **-ëll** and **-ull** are not, except in monosyllabics.

7. Endings in **-ua**, **-uall**, **-iell** and **-yell** are stressed on the first vowel of the diphthong. Because the vowel changes in declension, the stress is on the vowel which replaces the diphthong, thus the stress shifts from the penultimate to the final syllable of the stem.

8. For nouns ending in **-ur** and **-aur** see Part F.

9. The position of the stress may determine the Declension Group to which a noun belongs, as in the Third Declension, or in a few cases the Declension to which a noun of foreign origin belongs (as with **Méri** and **Ramó**). It may also distinguish between two apparently similar words, as in

   barí: *shepherd*, **bári**: *the grass,* **drejtóri**: *the director*, **drejtorí**: *directorate*.

XXVI USE OF CASES

1. The Nominative case is used:

a. To denote the subject of a sentence.

b. To indicate the complement of a sentence containing a verb such as *to be* or *to become*.

c. (In the Indefinite Form) As a form of address. It may be preceded by the particle **o** (or **oj**, for feminine nouns) in this usage, or the **o** (or **oj**) may be suffixed. This is a vestigial form of a former Vocative case.

d. After the prepositions **kah, nga** and **te (tek)**, when the noun will normally be in the Definite Form.

e. As the Citation Form.

2. The Accusative case is used:

a. To denote the direct object of a transitive verb.

b. In apposition, as a predicate. The direct object of the verb is an Object Clitic, and the noun indicates the effect of the verb. The Object Clitic itself may be followed by a noun in the Definite Accusative, also representing the direct object, which may be followed by a noun in the Indefinite Accusative:

E emëruan Alushin zëdhënës: *they nominated Alush as spokesman.*

c. Adverbially, to denote:

   i. The time or duration of an action.
   ii. Price or quantity.

Revista shitet një euro: *the magazine is sold for one euro.*

Ky paket peshon katër kilogramë: *this package weighs four kilograms.*

d. After the following locational prepositions:

Mbi, më, ndër, në, nën, nëpër, për, përmbi.

Generally the noun governed by these prepositions will be in the Indefinite Accusative, unless it is defined by an adjective or a following Genitive.

e. **Mbi** and **për** are also followed by the Accusative in their alternative meaning of *about*. Again the noun will be in the Indefinite Form unless defined by an adjective or following Genitive.

f. The prepositions **me**: *with* and **pa**: *without* are also followed by the Accusative. Again the noun will be in the Indefinite Form unless defined by an adjective or following Genitive, or unless it is a proper noun.

3. The Genitive, Dative and Ablative cases of the Indefinite Form may not be used without a definer, e.g. **një** (singular), **ca** or **disa** (plural) or demonstrative (**këtij/kësaj**, **atij/asaj**) except when the Ablative is used descriptively (see below) or after **prej**.

4. The Genitive case is used as in English:

a. To show ownership or possession or a strong connection with a preceding noun:

   Libri i mesuesit: *the teacher's book.*

b. As a definer of the principal noun, where the noun in the Genitive case has a function comparable to that of an adjective.

   Gramatika e gjuhës shqipe: *the grammar (-book) of the Albanian language.*

   Biblioteka e Gjilanit: *the Gjilan library.*

   Komuna e Sharrit: *the Sharr municipality.*

c. Partitively.

d. To convey an adjectival meaning: **i/e fundit**: *last.*

e. As the subject or object of a deverbal noun. After deverbal nouns formed from transitive verbs, the second noun is the object of the action described, but is the subject of an intransitive deverbal noun.

f. After certain prepositional phrases:

Me anë, nga ana, për shkak.

5. The Dative case is used:

a. To denote the indirect object of a sentence:

Bin Laden i ofron zjarrpushim Evropës: *Bin Laden offers Europe a ceasefire* (**Kosova sot**).

Ia tregoi faturën inspektorit: *he showed the invoice to the inspector.*

b. To indicate a person affected in some way by the action described in a verb or participle, such as:

i. Dative of Advantage as in:

t'u mundësojë komunave që të marrin rolin udhëheqes: *to enable municipalities to take a leading role* (**Koha ditore**).

ii. Dative of Disadvantage as in:

Tritoli i ka marrë jetën 61-vjeçarit: *TNT killed* (deprived of life) *a 61-year old man.* (**Ballkan**).

6. The uses of the Ablative Case are generally similar to those of the Genitive, the difference generally being that where no preposition is used to link two nouns, both nouns will generally be in the Indefinite Form, and the second noun in the Ablative. There is no interchangeability where a preposition is used, that is to say that prepositions will govern either the Ablative case or the Genitive case. The use of the two forms of the Indefinite Ablative plural is set out at IV 5 b.

The Ablative case is used:

a. After prepositions such as **prej**, **afër**, **jashtë**.

i. A noun may be used in the Indefinite Ablative form after **prej** without any definer such as **një**.

ii. With place-names **prej** is followed by the Indefinite Form, as in **prej Prizreni**: *from Prizren*.

b. To indicate the origin, nature or composition of the preceding noun:

verë Therande: *wine from Theranda*, **mish lope**: *beef*.

In this usage the preceding noun will be in the Nominative or Accusative Case of the Indefinite Form, and the qualifying noun will be in the Indefinite Ablative. If the preceding noun has any case inflection or is in the Definite Form, then the (Definite) Genitive construction must be used.

c. Partitively, as in: **Gjysmë ore**: *half an hour*.

d. After **njefarë**: *some kind of* (in the singular), **lloj-lloj**: *all sorts of* and **gjithfarë**: *all sorts of* (in the plural), when the noun will be in the Indefinite Form.

e. Adjectivally, using the **-sh** form when plural:

Mollë sherri: *bone of contention* (cf. German *Zankapfel*), **frizer meshkujsh**: *gentlemen's hairdresser*, **treni mallrash**: *goods train*, **lule pranvere**: *primrose* (singular), *spring flowers* (plural).

f. Adverbially: **maleve**: *in the mountains*, **rrugës**: *along the road*, **verës**: *in summer*.

XXVII   **PREFIXES AND ANTONYMS**

1. Nominal prefixes used in Albanian can be classed as:

a. Those which create antonyms, such as **mos-** and **pa-**.

b. Adverbs such as **mbi-, nën-, para-, pas-** and **për-**, the meaning of which is generally obvious, e.g. **parafolës**: *previous speaker*, **mbikalim**: *flyover*, **nënkolonel**: *lieutenant-colonel*, **pranverë**: *spring*.

c. **Stër-**, which is discussed below.

d. Other prefixes of Greek or Latin origin, which in some instances are used before words of Albanian origin, as in **ultravjollcë**: *ultraviolet,* **infrakuq**: *infrared*.

2. **Mos-** is used with deverbal nouns to create antonyms, such as **mosçmim**: *disregard, underestimation*, **mosnjohje**: *ignorance, non-acceptance*.

3. **Pa-** is used with abstract nouns to create antonyms, such as **padrejtësi**: *injustice*, **pavetëdije**: *unconsciousness*.

4. **Ç-** is not generally used to form noun antonyms. Nouns with this prefix are derived from antonymous verbs. An exception is **çekuilibër**: *imbalance*.

5. **Stër-** is primarily used with nouns denoting relatives to indicate a further generation, as in **stërgjysh**: *great-grandfather*, **stërnip**: *great-nephew/ great-grandson*.

6. **Stër-** can also indicate abnormality or excess, as in **stërdhëmbë**: *snaggletooth* and **stërhollës**: *hair-splitter* (a person who goes into excessive detail).

7. **Suficit**: *surplus* is the antonym of **deficit**: *deficit*.

8. The antonym of **opozitë**: *Opposition* (political), is **pozitë**: *the party/ies in power*. This term is used in Local Government, to avoid confusion with **qevëria**, but may also be used to refer to a national government.

    Opozita bëri vërejtje, pozita u shpreh e kënaqur: *the opposition made observations, the party in power declared itself satisfied* (**Koha ditore**, about Gjakova).

9. The antonym of **stabilitet**: *stability* is **destabilitet**: *instability* (**Epoka e re**) from the verb **destabilizoj**.

10. The antonym of **nivel**: *level* is **disnivel**: *disparity, difference*, as in **kalim me disnivelë**: *crossing* (road-road or road-rail) *with bridge or flyover*.

XXVIII NOUN FORMATION BY SUFFIX 1: AGENT NOUNS AND NOUNS OF ORIGIN

1. Albanian uses a wide variety of suffixes to form nouns denoting occupation, residence or origin, both from other nouns and from other parts of speech. The suffixes listed here are all stressed, except **-ës**: nouns with these suffixes form feminine forms with **-e**.

2. Certain suffixes are found more frequently with words which are recognisably derived from other languages.

3. The suffix **-s** or **-ës** is used after verb stems to describe someone who performs an action. It is usually added to the participle form, as in **mësues**: *teacher* using the

Gheg participle **mësue**, **nxënës**: *pupil*, and **shitës**: *salesman*: the present stem is used in **vrasës**: *killer*.

4. This suffix may also be used after nouns to denote a person who performs an action relating to that noun, as in **gjykatës**: *judge*, whose functions are performed **në gjykatë**: *in court*.

5. The suffixes **-ar**, **-tar** and **-atar** usually describe a person by his activity or occupation: examples are **gazetar**: *journalist,* **harkëtar**: *archer,* **shkrimtar**: *writer* and **zdrukthëtar**: *carpenter*. These suffixes are all productive, i.e. still used to form new words.

6. The suffix **-ar** can also be used to indicate origin or nationality, as in **kosovar**: *inhabitant of Kosova* and **gjakovar**: *inhabitant of Gjakova*. For other suffixes denoting residence or origin see Section XLI.

7. The suffix **-or** is usually descriptive, but is sometimes found in nouns denoting origin, as in **malësor**: *mountain dweller*. This and the suffix **-tor**, as in **punëtor**: *worker*, are both non-productive.

8. With words of obvious foreign origin the following (stressed) suffixes may be found:

    -ant as in **kursant**: *course participant,* **-ier/-er** as in **bankier**: *banker,* **-ist** as in **sportist**: *athlete* or *sportsman* and **-ik** as in **alkoolik**: *alcoholic*.

9. The suffix **-er** is found in words of English origin ending in *-er*, e.g. **trainer**: *trainer,* **lider**: *leader,* **ploter**: *plotter* (instrument), also in **konduktor**: *(bus-) conductor,* **shofer**: *chauffeur*. In **noter**: *Notary* it represents the French ending *-aire*. The collective or abstract noun is therefore, as in French, **notariat**.

10. The suffix **-ist** can be used to denote followers of a movement or philosophy. While it is generally found after words of foreign origin, it can also be used with words of Albanian origin as in **majtist**: *left-winger*.

11. The suffix **-xhi** (or **-çi**) of Turkish origin is no longer productive, but is found in words such as **hanxhi**: *innkeeper* and **qiraxhi**: *tenant*. It increasingly has a pejorative implication, as in **kalemxhi**: *scribbler, hack writer*, and **hallvaxhi**, which can mean *halva-seller* or *slipshod worker*. The **çi** form of the suffix is used with words ending in an unvoiced consonant, e.g. **sahatçi**: *watchmaker*.

XXIX NOUN FORMATION BY SUFFIX 2: INANIMATE (CONCRETE) NOUNS

1. While many nouns denoting inanimate objects have ancient etymological roots, others are recognisably derived from other words, usually nouns or verbs, by the addition of a suffix, and there is generally a link between the suffix and the meaning. Only those suffixes which have specific meanings are discussed here. For a more detailed treatment the reader should consult Standard Albanian (see bibliography).

2. The suffixes **-ës** and **-ëse** indicate tools or instruments, as **çelës**: *key* (from **çel**: *I open*) or objects performing a function such as **ndenjës**: *seat* from **ndenjur**: *sat*.

3. The suffix **-ishtë/ishte** denotes the place where something is grown or occurs, such as **fidanishte**: *tree nursery*, i.e. place for saplings (**fidan**: *sapling*).

4. The suffix **-óre/-tóre** denotes the place at which a substance is worked upon, sold or otherwise exploited, or an activity takes place. Examples include **avokatore**: *lawyer's office*, **barnatore**: *pharmacy*, **bletore**: *apiary* and **ëmbëltore**: *confectioner's shop*. In **gropore**: *little hole* it has a diminutive effect.

5. The suffix **-sirë/ësirë/ëtirë** is used to create nouns from adjectives and verbs, for example:

   ëmbëlsirë: *sweet food, dessert,* **hapësirë**: *open space.*

6. The suffixes **-ishte** and **-urina** form plural nouns with a collective meaning, such as **mbeturina**: *leftovers*, **qelqurina**: *glassware* and **barishte**: *herbs*. Where the noun ends in **-ur**, the suffix is telescoped to **-ina**.

XXX NOUN FORMATION BY SUFFIX 3: ABSTRACT NOUNS

1. There are many abstract nouns derived from other parts of speech, primarily verbs and adjectives. They form three main groups:

a. Deverbal nouns, which are discussed separately in the next Section.

b. Those with the suffixes **-i**, **-ëri** and **-ësi**, which are feminine in gender.

c. Those formed with suffixes of foreign origin, of which the majority is masculine in gender.

2. Most other abstract nouns, which can be derived from nouns, adjectives or adverbs, end with the suffix **-i,**

-ëri or -ësi. All abstract nouns with these endings are feminine. **Zotëri**: *lord* appears to be an abstract noun derived from **zot**: *master* but is used as a masculine noun, and also as a respectful term of address. It declines in Group 4 of the Third Declension.

3. The suffix -i is generally used after participles ending in -ur such as **njohuri**: *knowledge* and **pasuri**: *wealth*, and also other nouns and adjectives ending in -ër, such as **verbëri**: *blindness* from **i verbër**: *blind* and **dhelpëri**: *cunning* from **dhelpër**: *fox*. It is occasionally found after other endings, as in **befasi**: *suddenness*, **drejtori**: *the directorate* or *the directors*.

4. The suffix -ësi is most commonly used after adjectives ending in -ë, -ël and -ër, as well as those ending in a consonant other than -r and having the stress on the last syllable, as in **gjatësi**: *length* and **shurdhësi**: *deafness*.

5. It is also used to form abstract nouns from verbs and adverbs, such as **kënaqësi**: *pleasure*, **afërsi**: *closeness*, and the nouns **cilësi**: *quality* and **sasi**: *quantity* from the interrogative pronouns **cili**: *which?* and **sa**: *how much?*

6. The suffix -ëri is similar in use to -ësi. It is in particular used after adjectives ending in -shëm, as in **llojllojshmëri**: *variety* from **i llojllojshëm**: *variegated*, and **dobishmëri**: *profit* from **i dobishëm**: *useful*.

7. Many collective nouns ending in -ri or -ëri may have an inclusive aspect, as in **graria e fshatit**: *the womenfolk of the village*. Such a noun may also have an abstract meaning, such as **djalëri**: *boys* (in general), *the boys of the locality* and *boyhood*.

8. The suffix **-llëk** is of Turkish origin and is added to nouns of Turkish origin, often with a pejorative sense. examples are **budallallëk**: *foolishness* and **pazarllëk**: *haggling, swindling*. It may also be added to adjectives as in **bollë**: *abundant* which telescopes the stem ending into the suffix to form **bollëk**: *abundance*.

9. The suffixes **-izëm**, **-ist**, **-azh**, **-ikë** and **-urë** are used primarily with words of foreign origin. Nouns suffixed with **-ist** and **-izëm** have also been formed from Albanian words: examples are **majtizëm**: *leftism* and **zyrtarizëm**: *bureaucracy*.

10. Often more than one noun may be formed from a single stem, using different suffixes, and with different meanings.

XXXI NOUN FORMATION BY SUFFIX 4: DEVERBAL NOUNS

N.B. References to conjugations follow the standard classification. References to Verb Classes within the conjugations follow the classification set out in the companion volume: Albanian Grammar: Albanian Verbs Explained.

1. As well as the Gerunds discussed earlier, there are many deverbal nouns, i.e. nouns derived from verbs: they fall into three main categories: agents, actions, and perfected actions, or the results of actions. Nouns denoting actions are often used instead of the Gerund.

2. Agent nouns are dealt with in Section XXVIII.

3. Nouns denoting actions add endings to the verb stem which vary according to the stem:

a. Verbs of Classes 1 to 3 of the First Conjugation (the **punoj, rrëfej** and **shkruaj** classes) add **-im** to the last consonant of the stem, such as **fillim**: *beginning*, **rrëfim**: *narration*. Such nouns are grammatically masculine in the singular but, as do many inanimate nouns, become grammatically feminine in the plural.

b. First Conjugation verbs of Class 4 (**lyej** Class) add **-je** to the Participle, e.g. **lyer/lyerje**.

c. First Conjugation verbs of Classes 5-8, which have a participle stem ending in a consonant, e.g. **bler(ë)** and **mbajt(ur)**, add **-je** to that stem.

d. Verbs of the Second and Third Conjugations add **-je** to the participle stem. Where that stem ends in **-g** or **-n**, the suffix is **-ie**, as in **djegie**: *burning* and **rrënie**: *fall*.

e. **Ndenjje** (Definite **ndenjja**): *sitting, remaining seated* adds **-j** to a verb stem ending in a soft consonant, but **përgjigje** (Definite **përgjigjja**): *reply* does not, except in the Nominative Singular Definite **përgjigjja**.

f. These are not rigid rules, and not every verb forms a verbal noun according to the above patterns or at all. Indeed, in some instances nouns ending in **-im** or **-je** /**-ie** may denote completed actions.

4. Nouns denoting completed actions:

a. A common ending for First Conjugation verbs is **-esë**, as in **ftesë**: *summons,* **mbulesë**: *lid, cover*.

b. The suffix **-atë** is used with some First Conjugation verbs, e.g. **ligjëratë**: *lecture:* from **ligjëroj**. It is used with verbs (ending in **-oj**) of foreign origin to correspond to the verbal noun ending in *-ation* (or the corresponding ending in the language of origin) as in **administratë**: *administration.*

c. For many Second Conjugation verbs, and verbs of Classes 4 to 8 of the First Conjugation, the ending in **-je** may denote the result of an action, e.g. **blerje**: *purchase* (item purchased) and **veshje**: *clothing* (item put on). Thus such a deverbal noun may have or acquire a concrete meaning.

d. The ending **-më** is added to the Past Definite stems of Second Conjugation verbs which contract their stems in the Past Definite (Class 5a), such as **bërtas/brita/britmë**: *shout*, **kërcas/krisa/krismë**: *crack*, **këlthas/klitha/klithmë**: *scream.*

e. The ending **-më** is added to the second person plural stem of a few verbs, e.g. **ndih-/ndihmë**: *help.*

f. The ending **-imë** is used to denote completed actions where the Citation Form of the verb ends in **-ij** (or **-in**, for Impersonal verbs), such as **bubullin/bubullimë**: *thunder*.

5. A deverbal noun can be formed from a verb formed from a noun, as **emërim**: *appointment*, **sendërtim**: *realisation.*

6. These notes do no more than illustrate ways in which nouns can be formed from verbs, and should not be taken as authority for the existence or precise meaning of a deverbal noun. Nor are all deverbal nouns formed in exact conformity with the principles set out above.

XXXII **NOUN FORMATION BY SUFFIX 5: DIMINUTIVES**

1. The main suffixes which convey a diminutive meaning are **-th** (for masculine nouns) and **-z** (or **-ëz**) and **-zë** for feminine nouns. Diminutives normally retain the gender of the original noun. Examples are:

   djalëth: *little boy*, **yllth**: *asterisk*, **lulëz**: *little flower*, **shtëpizë**: *little house*.

2. The suffix **-ush** is used to denote young animals, as in **dhelpërush**: *foxcub*.

3. **Mi**: *mouse* has diminutives **miúsh** (male) and **miúshe** (female).

4. **Qytezë**: *small town* formed from the masculine noun **qytet**: *town* is feminine.

XXXIII **NOUN FORMATION BY SUFFIX 6: PEJORATIVES**

1. The suffixes **-ac**, **-acák** are used to denote a person who has an undesirable characteristic, such as **frikacak**: *coward* (from **frikë**: *fear*), or a person lacking a normal feature, such as **dorac**: *one-armed man*. By contrast **doracak** means *handbook*.

2. Other, rarely used, suffixes with similar meaning are:

   -aláq, -alúq, -aléc, -amán, -arásh, -avéc.

Relatively commonly found pejoratives are **barkalec**: *big-bellied man* and **grindavec**: *quarrelsome person*.

3. The suffix **-ok** may have a pejorative meeting, as in **mjeshtërok**: *poor* (i.e. unskilful) *craftsman*, **malok**: *hillbilly*.

XXXIV FORMATION OF FEMININE COUNTERPARTS

1. The masculine and feminine of any species are distinguished either by suppletive forms, as with most members of the family, or by suffixes.

2. In a very few instances the male and female words for a specified individual have the same CF, but separate declined forms. Examples are:

thjeshtër: *stepchild*, **vjehërr**: *parent- in- law*.

3. With members of the family, there is usually no morphological relationship between the two forms:

Masculine		Feminine	
baba	*father*	**nënë**	*mother*
vëlla	*brother*	**motër**	*sister*
nip	*nephew/ grandson*	**mbesë**	*niece/ grand-daughter*
dhëndër	*son-in-law*	**nuse**	*daughter-in-law*
djalë	*son*	**vajzë**	*daughter*

4. By contrast **bir**: *son* and **bijë**: *daughter* have an obvious resemblance, and **gjyshe**: *grandmother* is formed from **gjysh**: *grandfather* by suffixation. Likewise **shoq**: *husband* and **shoqe**: *wife*.

5. Suffixes are used to indicate that a noun is the female counterpart of a male. The most common is **-e**, as in:

mjek	*doctor*	**mjeke**
gjysh	*grandparent*	**gjyshe**
mik	*friend*	**mike/mikeshë**
fshatar	*villager*	**fshatare**
tiranas	*person from Tirana*	**tiranase**

6. The suffix **-eshë** is found in **luan/luaneshë**: *lion (ess)*, **drejtor/drejtoreshë**: *director,* **baroneshë**: *baroness*. Sometimes the male plural suffix (or part of it) precedes the **eshë**, as in **Mbretëreshë**: *Queen*, **bejlereshë**: *wife or daughter of a bey* and **ustalleshë**: *master craftswoman, crafty woman*.

7. The suffix **-ë** is found in the following:

Masc. Sing.	Meaning	Fem. Sing.	Fem. Pl.
breshk #	*turtle*	**breshkë**	**breshka**
fqinj #	*neighbour*	**fqinjë**	**fqinja**
kunat	*brother-in-law*	**kunatë**	**kunata**
njerk #	*stepfather*	**njerkë**	**njerka**
plak	*old man*	**plakë**	**plaka**
stërqok #	*jackdaw*	**stërqokë**	**stërqoka**
zog	*bird*	**zogë**	**zoga**

a. Nouns marked # confusingly form the (masculine) plural with **-ë**.

b. There are differences between the secondary meanings of **hut**: *hoot owl* and its feminine counterpart **hutë**.

8. The feminine form of **kushëri**: *cousin* is **kushërirë**.

9. The suffix **-ushë** is used to denote the female of certain species: **drenushë**: *doe* and **arushë**: *she-bear*.

10. The suffix **-onje** is obsolete and only found in **ujkonje**: *she-wolf*.

11. **Gjerak**: *falcon* has feminine form **gjeraqinë**.

12. **Kukuvriq** and **kukuvajkë**, both referring to owl species, do not correspond exactly in meaning.

13. Other suffixes used are:

    a. **-icë** as in **buallicë**: *buffalo-cow*.

    b. **-kë** as in **çobankë**: *shepherdess*.

14. With most domestic animals the masculine and feminine nouns are completely unrelated (π indicates the form more generally used to refer to the species):

Masculine		Feminine	
cjap	*(billy)goat*	**dhi**	*(nanny)goat*
dash	*ram*	**dele**	*ewe*
gjel	*rooster*	**pulë** π	*hen*
ka	*ox*	**lopë** π	*cow*
kalë π	*stallion*	**pelë**	*mare*
qen	*dog*	**bushtër**	*bitch*
derr	*pig*	**dosë**	*sow*

XXXV <u>MASCULINE COUNTERPARTS</u>

For some species of fauna a suffix is added to form the masculine noun. Examples include:

galë	*daw*	**gallof**	*jackdaw*
macë	*cat*	**maçok**	*tomcat*
mëllenjë	*blackbird*	**mëllenjan**	*blackbird*
patë	*goose*	**patok**	*gander*
rosë	*duck*	**rosak**	*drake*
skile	*vixen*	**skilak**	*dog-fox*

XXXVI   **AUNTS AND UNCLES**

1. The English words *uncle* and *aunt* describe relations on both sides of the family, and relations by marriage as well as blood relations. Albanian speakers make distinctions:

axhë	*father's brother*) both Third
dajë	*mother's brother*) Declension
dajeshë	*wife of* **dajë**
hallë	*father's sister*, or *wife of* **axhë** or **dajë**
teze	*mother's sister*
ungj	*father's or mother's brother*
xhaxhá	*father's brother* (same as **axhë**)
xhaxheshë	*wife of* **xhaxha**

2. Other relations (but see also Section XX) include:

baxhanak)	*brother-in-law*	**dadë**	*older sister*
mjeshtak)	(*husband of wife's sister*)	**tezak**	*cousin* (*son of* **teze**)
bacë	*older brother*	**thjeshtër**	*Stepchild* (m. or f.)

XXXVII   **FORMATION OF OTHER PARTS OF SPEECH FROM NOUNS**

1. Nouns can be used to form other parts of speech, such as adjectives, adverbs, verbs and prepositions, in addition to their use in phrases.

2. Many adjectives ending in **-ësh** are formed by compounding numbers and nouns, such as **dykrerësh**: *two-headed*. The ending is **-ësh** regardless of the plural form of the noun, as in:

katërkatësh: *four-storied* from **kate**, and **8 bitësh**: *8-bit* from **bita**: (computer) *bits*.

3. Many nouns are also used as adjectives; a few (indeclinable) adjectives are formed by doubling nouns, such as **kuti-kuti**: *chequer-patterned* and **vija-vija**: *striped*.

4. For more on formation of adjectives from nouns, see Part B, Section XI.

5. Various suffixes are used to form adverbs from nouns: **-as, -azi, -thi** and **-çe** are among the more common.

6. Adverbs can also be formed from reduplicated nouns, as in **herë-herë**: *at times*, **palë-palë**: *in pairs* and **cuka-cuka**: *little by little*.

7. Verbs can be formed from nouns by suffixation, by prefixation, by a combination of both, or by simply conjugating the noun stem. Most new verbs, and all new verbs derived from foreign words, are created by adding the suffix **-o**, thus creating verbs of the **punoj** Class. More than one verb can be formed from a noun, as in **emëroj**: *nominate* and **emërtoj**: *name*.

8. Other suffixes forming verbs in the **punoj** Class are **-ro, -so** and **-to** as in **lajmëroj**: *I inform*, **punësoj**: *I employ* and **copëtoj**: *I break up*.

9. In the past the **-os** suffix (sometimes **-atos**) was commonly added to nouns. Some **-os** verbs have pairs with the **-o** suffix, and some with the **-is** suffix.

10. Prefixation is seen in **përdor**: *use*, **çmend**: *madden*.

11. **Kripë**: *salt* becomes **krip**: *I salt*.

12. Prepositions formed from nouns can be:

a. Simple derivations, as in **ballë**: *opposite*, where the noun appears unaltered, compound, as in **përballë**: *opposite* and **krahas**: *alongside*, where the nouns have a prefix and suffix respectively.

b. Phrasal, where the noun appears as part of a phrase, as in **me anë**: *by means of* and **për shkak**: *because of.* Phrasal prepositions generally govern the Accusative or Genitive cases, whereas the other types formed from nouns govern the Ablative.

13. These notes set out general principles. The reader should always check in a dictionary whether a possible derivative exists, and whether it has any particular meaning.

XXXVIII **RELATIONSHIP OF MEANING AND FORM**

1. There are many instances in the Albanian language where there is a link between the lexical meaning of a noun and its grammatical characteristics. The general principle is that animate nouns correspond in gender to the being which they designate, except for those animal species where gender is of no economic importance, i.e. where the labour, offspring, eggs, milk or skin are of no commercial importance. Examples are **baldosë**: *badger* and **mëllenjë**: *blackbird*. The grammatical gender of an inanimate noun is determined by its form.

2. The most obvious example is a masculine proper name such as **Kolë** or **Ramë** which declines as a feminine noun yet, because it denominates a male

being, has masculine gender, requiring adjectives and pronouns referring to it to be masculine.

3. Equally there is a group of masculine nouns denoting relatives and other male beings which belongs to the Third Declension but is masculine grammatically.

4. Some feminine names such as **Antigon** decline as masculine nouns but are grammatically feminine.

5. The form and grammatical gender of animate nouns depend on the gender of the being described, except for animal species of no commercial importance. For these the grammatical gender is therefore determined by the form rather than the meaning.

6. Many suffixes denoting agents are stressed, thus nouns with such suffixes can form the plural with -**ë**. Some descriptive suffixes such as -**ak** are stressed, but others are not, hence such nouns as **prishtinas** and **mësues** cannot take an -**ë** to form the plural.

7. Masculine Nouns forming the plural in -**e**, which are almost all inanimate, become grammatically feminine in the plural. So too do many nouns which form the plural with -**ra**.

8. As well as indicating (often but not always) a change of gender in the plural of masculine nouns, the ending -**ra** often indicates a change of meaning to *"types of,"* or *"large quantities of,"* as in the case of substance nouns (both masculine and feminine) which cannot logically have a plural, e.g.:

Në ujëra jetojnë gjysma e të gjitha të kafshëve të njohura: *half of the world's known creatures live in water* (**Zëri**.)

9. Some nouns denoting metals form a plural in **-a** which means *goods made of...*, as in **bakra**: *copperware*, **hekura**: *ironware* and **plumba**: *lead seals* or *bullets*.

10. Masculine nouns with certain singular stem endings (as listed in Plural Classes 6 and 7), with a few exceptions, take different suffixes to form the plural depending on whether the noun is animate or inanimate.

11. Different plural forms distinguish between the plurals of homonyms or show different shades or aspects of meaning in the plural of nouns with a single (possibly broad) meaning in the singular. A particularly good example is **element** from Class 6, where the regular plural endings for this Class (-**ë** for animates and -**e** for inanimates) are added to the singular homonyms.

XXXIX   FALSE FRIENDS

The English-speaking reader will come across many Albanian words which resemble English words, but in fact have a completely different meaning. Sometimes the meaning will be derived from a similar-looking French word, and sometimes from a German or Italian word. Some more commonly found False Friends (nouns and adjectives only) are listed in Part F.

XL   DAYS OF THE WEEK

These are feminine articulated nouns. The names of the various days are generally used on their own, but they can also be used with **dita**, as in **dita e hënës**

XLI NOUNS DENOTING ORIGIN OR RESIDENCE

Albanian uses a variety of suffixes to denote origin, residence and nationality. In some instances place-names with identical endings will use different suffixes. Some examples are listed below:

	Town/city/village	Region	Country
-ak	durrsak		austriak
-an	dibran		gjerman
-ar	korçar, gjakovar	gorar	
-as	prishtinas	kurveleshas	
-en			maroken
-ez			portugez
-i		devolli	
-ian			laosian
-ik			britanik
-it	gjirokastrit	zagorit	
-iot	mallakastriot		
-jan		llapjan	kuvajtjan
-jat	vlonjat		
-jot	himarjot		
-li	mamushali		
-or	mirditor/mirditas	zadrimor	
-tan	krutan		

XLII SURNAMES

1. Albanian surnames are almost invariably rendered in the Definite Form, and decline normally. They will retain the Definite Form even when preceded by a title, which may appear in either Definite or Indefinite Form. The name may be First or Second Declension, as in **Rexhepi** or **Binjaku**, or Third Declension, as

Berisha and **Qosja**, but the spelling and declension pattern of the surname remain the same regardless of the gender of the person bearing the name.

2. Surnames ending in -**e** and -**o** such as **Kadare** and **Karamelo** take Third Declension Definite endings when they are an integral part of a phrase or sentence, but otherwise remain in the Indefinite Form. **Kadare** is stressed on the last syllable, **Nano** on the penult.

3.a. Surnames ending in -**j** do not take a suffix in forming the Nominative Definite Singular. They take the endings -**n** and -**t** in the Accusative and Oblique cases in accordance with normal declension patterns, as in:

   Nga ana e Adem Çollakajt, sipas E. Çabejt.

b. Endings -**un** and -**ut** are sometimes (incorrectly) seen.

4. Surnames used in the plural decline normally, as in:

   në lagjen e Jasharëve: *in the area where the Jashari family lives*.

5. Foreign surnames are often accompanied by a title, and therefore left in the Indefinite Form. When used on their own they are often seen in the Indefinite Form, although correctly they take the Definite Form.

XLIII GEOGRAPHICAL NAMES

1. Geographical names in Albanian can be either masculine or feminine. The gender will usually be apparent from the ending. All names ending in -**ë** are feminine, with very few exceptions.

2. Foreign place-names rendered in Albanian cannot be readily classified as to declension forms and gender. Each one should be checked individually

3. Names of countries or regions ending in -i, such as **Shqipëri**: *Albania*, **Kroaci**: *Croatia*, **Çamëri**: *Chameria* are feminine: some are clearly collective nouns.

4. The gender of compound geographical names such as **Mali i Zi**, **Bregu i Fildishtë**, **Gadime e Poshtme** or **Qafa e Zhurit** is evident from the principal noun.

5. With simple names ending in -**ël**, -**ër** and -**i** the gender is not obvious from the Indefinite Form.

6. Within Albania, the comprehensive listing found in **Fjalor i emrave gjeografikë të Republikës së Shqipërisë (Tirana 2002)** permits a few deductions to be made. The observations below relate only to simple names of towns, villages and other settlements.

a. Of names ending in -**í**, 46 are feminine, whereas 18 are masculine (4 First Declension, 14 Second Declension).

b. Names ending in -**ër**: 12 masculine, 14 feminine.

c. Names ending in -**ull**: 10 masculine, 4 feminine.

d. As regards names ending in -**ël**, -**ëm** -**ën**, -**ëz**, -**ur**, -**ul** no conclusions can be drawn.

e. The names of 5 settlements are feminine plural, e.g. **Gjegje** near **Kukës**, while **Gjazuj** is masculine plural.

7. Within the **troje shqiptare**:

a. **Hotël** (near **Kumanovë**) is feminine, and has Definite Form **Hotla**. Likewise **Duhël (Duhla)** near **Therandë**.

b. **Çabër, Dibër, Shkodër** and **Zhegër** are feminine: **Ohër** (town and lake) and **Ibër** (river) are masculine.

c. **Viti, Vushtrri, Abri** and **Hajvali** are all feminine, but the river **Dri** (Definite **Drini**) is masculine.

8. From elsewhere:

i. The following are feminine: **Zvicër**: *Switzerland*, **Akër**: *Accra*, **Londër**: *London*, **Flandër**: *Flanders* and **Sumatër**: *Sumatra*.

ii. The river **Tigër**: *Tigris* is masculine.

9. Place-names ending in **-aj, -ej** and **-oj** with the stress on or before the penultimate syllable such as **Ferízaj** and **Pétkaj** do not have a separate Nominative Definite Form. Where, however, the name is monosyllabic, as in **Xhaj**, or the stress is on a final syllable ending in vowel + **j**, as in **Biláj, Synéj** and **Surrój**, the name will follow the normal First Declension pattern.

10. While names ending in **-ël** and **-ër** such as **Hotël** and **Dibër** shed the **ë** of the last syllable, names ending in **-ës** such as **Durrës** and **Kukës** do not, although this sound is all but lost in the spoken form, and completely disappears in **durrsak**: *resident of Durrës, connected with or relating to Durrës*.

11. The name of a capital city is sometimes used with the adjective **zyrtar** to denote the government of the relevant country, as in **Shkupi zyrtar**: *the FYROM Government*.

PART B

ADJECTIVES

I **ELEMENTS OF ADJECTIVES**

1. Adjectives describe nouns, or, less frequently, pronouns. They agree in number, gender and case with the noun or pronoun to which they refer, and usually follow the noun. They can vary in degree, becoming Comparative or Superlative. In practice in Albanian many adjectives share the same forms for singular and plural forms, and some have identical masculine and feminine forms. Case can be determined only where the adjective is preceded by a Clitic which, when used before an adjective, is also known as an Adjectival Article. Stress does not alter during declension, except for **i madh/të mëdhenj** and **e madhe/të mëdha**.

2. Adjectives in Albanian are classified primarily as Articulated, i.e. preceded by a Clitic which agrees in Gender, Number, Case and Definiteness with the preceding noun, or Unarticulated, i.e. without a preceding Clitic. Unarticulated adjectives agree in Gender and Number with the preceding noun, but have no means of indicating agreement with either the Case or the Form (Definite or Indefinite) of the preceding noun.

3. Articulated adjectives are generally cited with the preceding Clitic **i** (in the dictionary entry placed after the adjective in brackets), and so it can be seen from the dictionary whether an adjective is articulated or not. Moreover there are certain rules which enable this to be determined.

4. A further classification must be made, based on the differences between simple, derived and compound adjectives. This distinction applies in determining the ADG to which an adjective belongs.

a. Simple adjectives usually describe an intrinsic feature of a noun, such as colour, size or age, such as **i gjatë**: *long, tall,* **i zi**: *black,* **i vjetër**: *old.*

b. Derived adjectives are relational, i.e. describe a characteristic of a noun by reference to something external, such as **i bësueshëm**: *reliable,* **librazhdas**: *from Librazhd.*

c. Compound adjectives consist of a noun plus adjective, two nouns, or two adjectives, and describe the noun by reference to the elements of the compound.

d. The three types are not separable into watertight divisions: **i vjetër** describes an intrinsic characteristic, but is derived from **vjet**: *years.* Equally **barkmadh**: *paunchy, gluttonous* may refer to an intrinsic physical feature or to an attitude towards food.

5. The various declension groups for adjectives do not coincide with the articulated and unarticulated categories. However since unarticulated adjectives have no preceding Clitic to indicate Gender, they generally indicate the feminine form by adding an ending, usually **-e**. Some groups of articulated adjectives also do this.

6. While generally the fact of being articulated or unarticulated is irrelevant to determining the ADG to which an adjective belongs, the following points may be considered:

a. Unarticulated adjectives which are not compounds form the feminine form with **-e** (ADG 1).

b. Most simple adjectives do not add endings except when forming the feminine plural with **-a** (ADG 2)**.**

7. The two principal forms of declension (regardless of articulation) are:

a. Identical singular and plural forms for both genders, with the feminine forms taking the ending **-e**: this is referred to as ADG 1.

b. Identical forms for masculine singular, feminine singular and masculine plural, with the feminine plural taking the ending **-a**: this is referred to as ADG 2.

8. Adjectives derived from nouns (without suffix, such as **trim**) take the same plural forms as the nouns, and the same suffixes to form the feminine but do not decline further. Examples are listed under ADG 4.

9. There are also some irregular adjectives.

10. Declension of compound adjectives is discussed at II 6, III 7-9 and IV 8 below.

II ARTICULATED ADJECTIVES

1. There are seven distinct categories of articulated adjectives, as set out below. In each case the ADG to which the category belongs is specified.

2. The first category consists of derived adjectives with the following suffixed endings: **-ëm, -m, -më, -shëm**.

a. These adjectives form the feminine by altering the Clitic to the feminine form (varying as to Case), adding -e and, where present, dropping the ë from the final syllable. They do not have separate plural endings, and so the plural is indicated only by the plural form of the Clitic. Examples are: **i këndshëm / e këndshme**: *pleasant*, **i nesërm/ e nesërme**: *tomorrow's*, **i tejmë/ e tejme**: *further*, **i mishtormë/ e mishtorme**: *fleshy*.

b. The declension is set out as ADG 1.

c. Note that **i njomë**: *wet* belongs to ADG 2, since it is a simple adjective, i.e. the **më** ending is not a suffix.

3. The second category consists of simple adjectives with the following endings:

-ët, -më, -të.

a. These alter the preceding Clitic to the Feminine form, but the adjective itself remains unaltered. Again there are no separate plural endings, and so the masculine plural is indicated only by the plural form of the Clitic. The feminine plural takes the ending -a. Examples:

b. **I dobët / e dobët**: *weak*, **i njomë/ e njomë**: *wet*.

c. The declension is set out in ADG 2.

4. The third category consists of simple adjectives ending in ë, such as **i bardhë**: *white*, **i parë**: *first*.

a. The preceding Clitic takes the Feminine form, but the adjective itself remains unaltered. As the masculine plural has no ending, the plural form is indicated only by the plural form of the Clitic. The feminine plural is formed with **-a**, dropping the final **-ë**.

b. These adjectives form part of ADG 2.

c. When used as the predicate of a clause or sentence, i.e. after a link verb such as *to be* or *to become*, a few adjectives of this group are used in unarticulated form, in particular **gjallë, sëmurë, shëndoshë**: Example:

u kthefsh shëndoshë: *may you return in good health*

d. Otherwise, when used predicatively, adjectives of this group take the "Indefinite" form of the Clitic, as set out in Section IX.

5. Category four consists of adjectives formed directly from participles, such as **i shkruar**: *written*, **i hapur**: *open* and **i zënë**: *occupied*.

a. These do not take endings in the feminine singular and masculine plural forms, but drop the final **-ë** and add **-a** to form the feminine plural.

b. These adjectives form part of ADG 2.

6. The fifth category consists of all compound adjectives formed by the preposition **pa**: *without* and a noun, as **i papunë/ e papunë**: *unemployed*.

Being invariable these belong to ADG 6, with two exceptions:

i pashoq/ e pashoqe: *peerless* (ADG 1, and with palatalisation of **shok** to **shoq**), **i pazoti/ e pazonja**: *inept*.

7. The sixth category consists of a small number of derived adjectives ending in -ër, such as **i poshtër**: *base*, **i shurdhër**: *deaf*. These form part of ADG 2.

8. The seventh category consists of a small number of simple adjectives of an everyday nature, such as **i ëmbël**: *sweet*, **i vogël**: *small*. Most of this group are irregular and are shown individually in the Adjective Declension Tables below. Those which are regular belong to ADG 2, but **i kuq** belongs to ADG 1.

9. **Tjetër**: *other, next* is unarticulated and invariable in the singular but the (irregular) plural **të tjerë/ të tjera** is articulated. It may also be used as a pronoun, and as such has masculine and feminine declensions.

III UNARTICULATED ADJECTIVES

1. Unarticulated adjectives fall into nine categories, and are nearly all either compound or derived. Most, but not all, have, in the absence of a Clitic, a distinct feminine form with the ending -e.

2. The first category comprises all adjectives showing origin or nationality, such as **prishtinas**: *(person) from Prishtina*, **vlonjat**: *(person) from Vlora*, **holandez**: *Netherlander*.

    These adjectives form part of ADG 1.

3. The second category consists of adjectives derived from participles by addition of the suffix -**ës** or -**s**, such as **shkatërrues**: *destructive*.

    These adjectives form part of ADG 1.

4. The third category consists of some simple adjectives, and adjectives derived from nouns by the addition of a suffix such as **-ar, -tar, -ik, -ist, -iv, -or, -tor**. These adjectives form the feminine singular and plural by adding -**e**, and the masculine plural by adding -**ë**. Examples are:

    abstrakt/abstrakte, plural **abstraktë/abstrakte**.

    These adjectives belong to ADG 3

5. The fourth category consists of adjectives which can also be used as nouns, such as **trim**: *bold*, **binjak**: *twin* and **dinjak**: *cunning*. Many of these use the suffix -**e** to indicate the feminine form, and form the plural in the same way as their corresponding nouns. These which form the plural with -**ë** belong to ADG 3: others belong to ADG 2, 4 or 5.

6. The fifth category consists of adjectives derived from nouns ending in **-çi, -li** and **-xhi**. These belong to ADG 4.

7. The seventh category consists of adjectives which are invariable, and therefore belong to ADG 6.

8. The sixth category consists of compound adjectives, where the second element of the compound is an adjective. These compounds follow the pattern of the adjective which forms the second part of the compound. An example is **kokëfortë**: *headstrong* which forms feminine plural **kokëforta**. Compound adjectives formed with irregular adjectives such as **i madh** follow the pattern of the adjective in question.

9. The eighth category consists of compound adjectives where the second element is a masculine noun (other

than a substance noun), or where a masculine noun is suffixed with **-ç** or **-ësh**, as for example **dykatësh**: *two-storied*. These adjectives belong to ADG 1. **Kokëderr**: *pig-headed* has the feminine form **kokëderre**, that is to say that the noun **derr**, which forms the second element, takes a suffix rather than being replaced by its feminine counterpart **dosë**.

10. The ninth category consists of compound adjectives where the second element is a feminine noun or a substance noun, such as **hundëshkabë**: *hook-nosed* and **gojëmjaltë**: *sweet-tongued*. and also compound adjectives including masculine nouns with unusual plural endings, such as **shpirtlepur**: *timorous* and **gjoksshkëmb**: *steadfast*. **Gojëmjaltë** does not add endings and therefore belongs to ADG 6. Likewise **hundëshkabë**. Declension patterns for some compound adjectives are set out on Page 201.

IV   ADJECTIVE DECLENSION TABLES

1. ADG 1 consists of adjectives which add **-e** to mark the feminine forms but do not have separate endings in either gender for the plural forms. The form of the clitic is determined by the gender, number and case and Form (Definite or Indefinite) of the preceding noun. An example is declined below:

    a.   Definite

Case	M. Singular.	F. Singular.
Nominative	**i djeshëm**	**e djeshme**
Accusative	**e djeshëm**	**e djeshme**
Gen/Dat/Abl	**të djeshëm**	**së djeshme**

Case	M. Plural	F. Plural.
Nominative	**e djeshëm**	**e djeshme**
Accusative	**e djeshëm**	**e djeshme**
Gen/Dat/Abl	**të djeshëm**	**të djeshme**

b. Indefinite

Case	M. Singular.	F. Singular.
Nominative	**i djeshëm**	**e djeshme**
Accusative	**të djeshëm**	**të djeshme**
Gen/Dat/Abl	**të djeshëm**	**të djeshme**

	M.Plural.	F. Plural
All Cases	**të djeshëm**	**të djeshme**

2. ADG 2 comprises those adjectives which do not require endings for the masculine plural or feminine singular forms, but mark the feminine plural with **-a**.

a. Adjectives ending in a consonant other than those ending in **-ël** and **-ër** decline as follows:

i. Definite

Case	M. Singular.	F. Singular.
Nominative	**i dobët**	**e dobët**
Accusative	**e dobët**	**e dobët**
Gen/Dat/Abl	**të dobët**	**së dobët**

Case	M. Plural	F. Plural.
Nominative	**e dobët**	**e dobëta**
Accusative	**e dobët**	**e dobëta**
Gen/Dat/Abl	**të dobët**	**të dobëta**

ii. Indefinite

Case	M. Singular.	F. Singular.
Nominative	**i dobët**	**e dobët**
Accusative	**të dobët**	**të dobët**
Gen/Dat/Abl	**të dobët**	**të dobët**

	M. Plural.	F. Plural
All Cases	**të dobët**	**të dobëta**

b. Adjectives ending in **-ël** and **-ër** (except for **i vogël** and **bistër**) decline as follows:

i. Definite

Case	M. Singular.	F. Singular.
Nominative	**i ëmbël**	**e ëmbël**
Accusative	**e ëmbël**	**e ëmbël**
Gen/Dat/Abl	**të ëmbël**	**së ëmbël**

Case	M.Plural.	F. Plural
Nominative	**e ëmbël**	**e ëmbla**
Accusative	**e ëmbël**	**e ëmbla**
Gen/Dat/Abl	**të ëmbël**	**të ëmbla**

ii. Indefinite

Case	M. Singular.	F. Singular.
Nominative	**i ëmbël**	**e ëmbël**
Accusative	**të ëmbël**	**të ëmbël**
Gen/Dat/Abl	**të ëmbël**	**të ëmbël**

	M.Plural.	F. Plural
All Cases	**të ëmbël**	**të ëmbla**

c. Adjectives and participles ending in -ë decline as follows:

i. Definite

Case	M. Singular.	F. Singular.
Nominative	**i zënë**	**e zënë**
Accusative	**e zënë**	**e zënë**
Gen/Dat/Abl	**të zënë**	**së zënë**

Case	M.Plural.	F. Plural
Nominative	**e zënë**	**e zëna**
Accusative	**e zënë**	**e zëna**
Gen/Dat/Abl	**të zënë**	**të zëna**

ii. Indefinite

Case	M. Singular.	F. Singular.
Nominative	**i zënë**	**e zënë**
Accusative	**të zënë**	**të zënë**
Gen/Dat/Abl	**të zënë**	**të zënë**

	M.Plural.	F. Plural
All Cases	**të zënë**	**të zëna**

3. ADG 3 consists of unarticulated adjectives which form the feminine (singular and plural) with -e and form the masculine plural with -ë. Many of these are also nouns. As there is no preceding clitic, the form of the adjective is varied only by Gender and Number: there is therefore no need to set out the full declension:

Masc. Sing	Fem Sing.	Masc Plural	Fem Plural
absolut	**absolute**	**absolutë**	**absolute**

4. ADG 4 consists of adjectives ending in **-çi**, **-li** and **-xhi**:

Masc. Sing	Fem Sing	Masc. Pl	Fem Pl
merakli	**merakleshë**	**meraklinj**	**meraklije**
qefli	**qefleshë**	**qeflinj**	
sojli	**sojleshë**	**sojlinj**	**sojlesha**

5. ADG 5 consists of nouns used as adjectives which take the same plural forms as the nouns themselves, but whose declension does not conform to the pattern of ADG 3 or ADG 4:

M. Sing.	F. Sing.	M. Pl.	F.Pl.
budalla	**budallaqe**	**budallenj**	as singular
fukara		**fukarenj**	
gegë	**gege**	**gegë**	**gege**
plak	**plakë**	**pleq**	**plaka**
trim	**trime**	**trima**	**trime**
turk	**turke**	**turq**	**turke**

Their meanings are respectively:

Crazy, poor, Gheg, old, brave, Turkish.

Trim has alternative feminine singular **trimëreshë**.

6. ADG 6 consists of adjectives which do not add suffixes to distinguish Gender or Number. This group includes adjectives formed by prefixing nouns with **pa-** (excluding **i pashok** and **i pazoti**). Examples are:

M. Sing.	F. Sing.	M. Pl.	F.Pl.	Meaning
bistër	**bistër**	**bistër**	**bistër**	*sour*
blu	**blu**	**blu**	**blu**	*blue*

M. Sing.	F. Sing.	M. Pl.	F.Pl.	Meaning
i fundit	e fundit	të fundit	të fundit	*last*
i pafé	e pafé	të pafé	të pafé	*impious*
i pafrikë	e pafrikë	të pafrikë	të pafrikë	*fearless*
i pafund	e pafund	të pafund	të pafund	*endless*
i pavënëre	e pavënëre	të pavënëre	të pavënëre	*unnoticed*
tralalá	tralalá	tralalá	tralalá	*hoity-toity*
gri	gri	gri	gri	*grey*
tabu	tabu	tabu	tabu	*taboo*

This group additionally includes the two adjectives **allafrënga**: *in Western European style* and **allaturka**: *in Turkish style, oriental*, and also adjectives formed by reduplication such as **copë-copë**: *fragmented*, **gropa-gropa**: *full of holes, pitted*, **kuti-kuti**: *chequer-pattern* and **vija-vija**: *striped*.

7. The following adjectives are irregular, as set out below:-

    i keq: *bad*, **i lig**: *evil*, **i madh**: *large*, **i ri**: *young*, **tjetër**: *other*, **i ve**: *widowed*, **i vogël**: *small*, **i zi**: *black*.

Masculine Singular	Feminine Singular	Masculine Plural	Feminine Plural
i keq	e keqe	të këqij	të këqija
i lig	e ligë	të ligj	të liga
i madh	e madhe	të mëdhenj	të mëdha
i ri	e re	të rinj	të reja
tjetër	tjetër	të tjerë	të tjera
i ve	e ve	të ve	të veja
i vogël	e vogël	të vegjël	të vogla
i zi	e zezë	të zinj	të zeza

8. The declension patterns of compound adjectives can be summarised as follows:

a. Masculine plural same as second element:

Description	CF Masculine Singular	Fem Sing	Mas Pl	Fem Pl
Noun plus masculine noun	**kokëderr**	e	a	e
	kokëkung(ull)	ulle	uj	ulle
Noun plus adjective	**gjakpirës**	e	-	e
Noun plus adjective	**zemërngushtë**	-	-	a
Noun plus irregular adjective	**zemërmadh**	as for **madh**		
Number plus noun plus -**sh**	**katërkohësh**	e	-	e
Quantity plus noun plus -**sh**	**shumëngjyrësh**	e	-	e
Noun plus adjective	**derëbardhë**	-	-	a

b. Masculine plural different from second element:

Description	CF Masculine Singular	note	Fem Sing	Mas Pl	Fem Pl
Adjective plus substance noun	**gojëmjaltë**	1	-	-	-
Adjective plus substance noun	**sylesh**	2	e	ë	e
Noun plus irregular noun	**gjoksshkëmb**	3	e	-	e
Noun plus feminine noun	**hundëshkabë**	4	-	-	-
Adjective plus masculine noun	**buzëgaz**	5	e	ë	e

201

Notes

1. **Gojëmjaltë** has as its second element **mjaltë**: *honey*, a typical masculine substance noun with vestigial neuter forms and plural in **-ra**.

2. **Sylesh**: *stupid* (literally *wool-eyed*), although formed from the substance noun **lesh**, adds **-e** to form the feminine form and **-ë** to form the masculine plural, thus deviating from the normal plural **leshra**.

3. **Gjokssshkëmb**: *steadfast* has as its second element **shkëmb**: *cliff* which forms plural **shkëmbinj**.

4. **Hundëshkabë**: *hook nosed* has as its second element a feminine noun, **shkabë**: *eagle*.

5. **Buzëgaz**: *cheerful* has as its second element **gaz**: *joy*, which does not normally have a plural form.

V   **AGREEMENT OF ADJECTIVES**

1. The general rule is that adjectives agree in Gender, Number and, where appropriate, Case with the noun or pronoun to which they refer.

2. Collective nouns, referring to a group or class of people, may be followed by an adjective in either single or plural form.

3. When the second person plural pronoun **Ju**: *you* is used to address an individual, any predicative adjective following may take the singular form.

4. If an adjective qualifies two or more nouns, it agrees in Gender, Number and Case with the last noun. Alternatively it may take the masculine plural form.

5. Although **vete**: *oneself* and its Definite Form **vetja** are feminine in form, a following adjective will take its gender from the noun or pronoun to which **vete** refers.

6. When qualifying a singular neuter noun, adjectives take the masculine form. The Adjectival Clitic follows the pattern set out in Part C at Section II 4.

   An example is **të kuqtë e madh**: *erysipelas*.

7. Adjectives qualifying neuter nouns in the plural take the feminine form.

8. The demonstrative **ky/kjo**: *this* takes the form **këta** when used before a singular neuter noun.

VI **COMPARISON OF ADJECTIVES**

1. Albanian adjectives can be varied by degree, in both directions. The positive comparisons (*more* and *most*) are made by prefixing the adverb **më**: *more, most*, while the diminishing comparisons are made using the adverbial phrase **më pak**: *less, least*.

2. The comparative form, e.g. **më i vjetër**: *older*, can be used with or without a noun. Where a noun is used it takes the Indefinite Form.

3. The superlative form, e.g. **më i vjetër**: *oldest*, can also be used with or without a noun. Where it is used with a noun, the noun takes the Definite Form, but the

particle **më** separates the noun and adjective, so that the Clitic preceding an articulated adjective will be in the "Indefinite" form. Where an adjective is used without a noun, the adjective will take the endings of the Definite Form.

VII   **POSITION OF ADJECTIVES**

1. Adjectives almost always follow the noun which they qualify: occasionally they will be placed before the noun for reasons of style.

2. When adjectives precede the noun they take endings identical to those of the Definite Form, with any **ë** which forms part of the Citation Form disappearing. The noun does not decline. As an example:

Singular

Case	Masculine	Feminine
Nom	**i forti ushtar**	**e bukura vajzë**
Acc.	**të fortin ushtar**	**të bukurën vajzë**
Gen.	**(i/e) të fortit ushtar**	**(i/e) së bukurës vajzë**
Dat./Abl	**të fortit ushtar**	**së bukurës vajzë**

Plural

Case	Masculine	Feminine
Nom/Acc	**të fortit ushtarë**	**të bukurat vajza**
Gen.	**(i/e)të fortëve ushtarë**	**i/e të bukurave vajza**
Dat./Abl	**të fortëve ushtarë**	**të bukurave vajza**

3. **I zi** becomes **i ziu, e ziun, të ziut, të zinjtë, të zinjve** when preposed, and **i ri** declines similarly.

4. Certain adjectives frequently precede the noun which they qualify, but <u>may</u> remain undeclined. These mostly denote "absolute" qualities, i.e. qualities which cannot be qualified by adverbs. Examples are:

I ashtuquajtur: *so-called*, **i njejtë**: *the same*, **i pare**: *first*, **i vetëm**: *only*, **të gjithë**: *all*, **tërë**: *entire*.

Liqeni mbante tërë kaltërsinë që ia jepte qielli: *the lake retained all the blueness which the sky gave it.* (Zija Çela, **Lëngata e Hënës**.)

5. Note set expressions such as:

Në të njejtën kohë: *at the same time*, **për të parën (dytën) herë**: *for the first (second) time*, but also **per herë të parë**.

VIII POSSESSIVE ADJECTIVES

1. Possessive adjectives have two forms of declension. The normal form, set out below, is used with most nouns, and the possessive follows the noun.

2. When referring to certain close relatives the possessive precedes the noun. The nouns concerned and the declension forms are given in Part A, at XX 2.

3. The possessive adjective when used without a noun becomes a pronoun, with endings based on those of the Definite Form. Pronouns are outside the scope of this work.

4. The normal declension is as follows: -

a. First person singular (*my*)

	Masc (s)	Fem. (s)	Masc (p)	Fem (p)
Nom.	im	ime	e mi	e mia
Acc	tim	time	e mi	e mia
Gen/Dat/Abl	tim	sime	të mi	të mia

b. Second person singular (*thy, yours* (familiar))

	Masc (s)	Fem.(s)	Masc (p)	Fem (p)
Nom.	yt	jote	e tu	e tua
Acc	tënd	tënde	e tu	e tua
Gen/Dat/Abl	tënd	sate	të tu	të tua

c. Third person singular (masculine subject)

	Masc (s)	Fem.(s)	Masc (p)	Fem (p)
Nom.	i tij	e tij	e tij	e tija
Acc	e tij	e tij	e tij	e tija
Gen/Dat/Abl	të tij	së tij	të tij	të tija

d. Third person singular (feminine subject)

	Masc (s)	Fem.(s)	Masc (p)	Fem (p)
Nom.	i saj	e saj	e saj	e saja
Acc	e saj	e saj	e saj	e saja
Gen/Dat/Abl	të saj	së saj	të saj	të saja

e. First person plural (*our*)

	Masc (s)	Fem.(s)	Masc (p)	Fem (p)
Nom.	ynë	jonë	tanë	tona
Acc	tonë	tonë	tanë	tona
Gen/Dat/Abl	tonë	sonë	tanë	tona

f.   Second person plural (*your*)

	Masc (s)	Fem.(s)	Masc (p)	Fem (p)
Nom.	juaj	juaj	tuaj	tuaja
Acc	tuaj	tuaj	tuaj	tuaja
Gen/Dat/Abl	tuaj	suaj	tuaj	tuaja

g.   Third person plural (*their*)

	Masc (s)	Fem.(s)	Masc (p)	Fem (p)
Nom.	i tyre	e tyre	e tyre	e tyre
Acc	e tyre	e tyre	e tyre	e tyre
Gen/Dat/Abl	të tyre	së tyre	të tyre	të tyre

5.   The reflexive possessive adjective is used with a third person subject to avoid ambiguity: it can of course be used only when the subject of the sentence and the possessor of the object referred to are the same, but can be used with singular or plural subjects.

	Masc (s)	Fem.(s)	Masc (p)	Fem (p)
Nom.	i vet	e vet	e vet	e veta
Acc	e vet	e vet	e vet	e veta
Gen/Dat/Abl	të vet	së vet	të vet	të veta

IX   ADJECTIVES USED PREDICATIVELY

1.   Adjectives used predicatively, i.e. following such verbs as **jam** and **bëhem**, will agree in gender and number with the subject of the sentence. If they are articulated, the Clitic will take the Indefinite Form, as for example:
studentët janë të lodhur: *the students are tired.*

2. When used predicatively after other verbs, articulated adjectives may lose their Clitic.

X   VERB-RELATED ADJECTIVES

1. The form of adjective which corresponds most closely to the Gerundive is formed:

a. From verbs of the **punoj** and **shkruaj** classes, by omitting the final **-ar** from the Participle and adding the ending **-eshëm/shme**, as in **i shpjegueshëm/ e shpjegueshme**: *explicable*.

b. From other verbs by removing the ending **-ur, -r** or **-rë** from the participle, as in **i djegshëm/ e djegshme**: *combustible*.

2. The following endings can be added to verb stems to form adjectives denoting capability or purpose: **-ues, -or, -tor**. These belong to ADG 3.

3. These notes do no more than illustrate ways in which adjectives can be formed from verbs, and should not be taken as authority for the existence of an adjectival derivative.

XI   ADJECTIVES FORMED FROM NOUNS

1. Some nouns can be used as adjectives. When used as adjectives they do not decline, but add an ending to denote the female form. This is usually **-e**, but if the original noun has a derived feminine form, e.g. **plak/ plakë**, then the feminine form of the adjective is similar to that of the noun. The plural of the adjective will be identical to that of the noun, in both masculine and feminine forms.

2. Many adjectives are formed by adding a suffix to a noun. Most common are: **-ar, -tar** and **-tor.**

3. The suffix **-ësh** is used to form adjectives from numbers and nouns, as **dhjetëkatësh**: *ten-storey*.

4. Adjectives can also be formed from nouns by prefixing the preposition **pa**: *without*, to indicate the lack or absence of the noun concerned in the person or object described by the adjective.

5. Certain expressions using the Genitive or Ablative of the noun have in effect become adjectives, often with a slightly altered meaning. Examples are:

    hiri: *grey* (literally *of ash*), **i udhës**: *necessary*, **i parafundit**: *penultimate*, **i fundit**: *last*.

6. Adjectives formed from nouns combined with verbs will usually be formed from the singular form, as in:

    dorëheqës: *resigning*, **paqeruajtës**: *peacekeeping*.

7. In many cases the noun in question will have only singular forms. **Golashënues**: *goal scoring* appears to have a plural noun, implying that the player scores many goals, but the **a** is arguably inserted for euphony. **Luftëranxitës**: *bellicose* (more commonly found as **luftënxitës**) is clearly plural.

XII NEGATION OF ADJECTIVES

1. To create a privative adjective, i.e. one indicating the lack of a given characteristic, which may or may not be an antonym, Albanian uses the prefixes **jo-**, **mos-** and **pa-**.

2. **Jo-** is used to create antonyms of existing unarticulated adjectives such as **jofetar**: *non-religious*. It is used both before words of Albanian origin and those of foreign origin.

3. **Mos-** is used before deverbal agent nouns, as in **mosbesues**: *sceptical*.

4. **Pa-** is used before other nouns, either as in **i pafaj**: *blameless* or, increasingly, with a suffix as in **i pafajshëm**, which has the same meaning. Whereas **jo-** is used before unarticulated adjectives, **pa-** must be used with articulated adjectives. Where **pa** is prefixed to a noun, the adjective thus formed is with two exceptions (**i pashoq** and **i pazoti**) invariable.

XIII **COLOURS**

1. Most of the colours in common use are articulated adjectives belonging to ADG 2, such as **i kaltër**: *blue*.

2. There are other less common unarticulated adjectives, such as **jeshil**: (*mallard*) *green* (ADG 1), **mavi**: (*dark*) *blue* (ADG 6), which may indicate the colour in general rather than a specific shade.

3. Many adjectives denoting non-primary colours are formed by compounding the noun **ngjyrë**: *colour* with a noun denoting an object of that colour, such as:

   ngjyrëkafe: *brown*, **ngjyrëtrëndafil**: *rose-coloured, pink*, **ngjyrëmanushaqe**: *violet*.

   Such adjectives are in general invariable and therefore belong to ADG 6.

PART C

CLITICS

I. **GENERAL**

1. Clitics are used in Albanian for the following purposes:

a. To link a noun in the Genitive Case with the (preceding) noun to which it refers, as in:

   qendra e qytetit: *the centre of the town.*

   vajza e Gencit: *Genc's daughter.*

b. To indicate the Gender and Case of an articulated adjective.

c. To distinguish participles when used as adjectives.

d. To articulate Substantivised Adjectives.

e. To denote neuter nouns, and in certain set expressions: in this usage only **të** and **së** are used.

f. As a third person possessive adjective preposed before nouns denoting close relatives and before **zot/zonjë**.

2. The uses a, b and c above are the most general, and although the parts of speech following the Clitic are different in these instances, the form and agreement of the Clitic are identical. They are therefore treated as identical.

3. The various declensions of the clitic are as follows:
a. Usages a b and c: see Section II below.

b. Usage d: see Noun Declension Tables in Part A, Sections XIII and XVI.

c. Usage e: see Part A Section VII.

d. Usage f: see part A Section XX.

4. When used before a neuter noun, the Clitic is invariably **të**, except in the set expression **me së** meaning *with* or *from* as in:

   Njeriu që nuk trillon ka pushuar me së jetuari: *the man who cannot tell a story has given up life* (**Zëri**).

5. The Clitic **së** is used to form adverbial phrases such as:

   së pari: *first*, **së fundi** *at last*, **së bashku**: *together*, **së paku**: *at least*.

6. The comparative adverb **më**: *more* intensifies the meaning, as in **më së fundi**: *at long last*, **më së paku**: *at the very least*.

II **DECLENSION TABLES**

1. Adjectival/Genitive Clitics have two forms of Declension, one form used when directly following a noun in the Definite Form, the other used in all other instances within a nominal phrase. Clitics used with preposed possessive adjectives have their own forms

as set out above. The use of the forms is discussed below. For convenience these are referred to as the Definite and Indefinite Forms. However because the use of the "Definite" Clitic is not entirely coincident with the use of the Definite Form of the noun, the words "Definite and "Indefinite" will be used with inverted commas when speaking of Clitics.

2. The "Indefinite Form" of the Clitic, i.e. that generally used (after a noun in the Indefinite Form, or when not directly following a Definite Noun) is as follows:

a. Singular

Case of preceding noun	Masculine	Feminine
Nominative	i	e
Accusative	të	të
Genitive	i/e të	i/e të
Dative/Ablative	të	të

b. Plural

Case of preceding noun	Masculine	Feminine
Nominative	të	të
Accusative	të	të
Genitive	i/e të	i/e të
Dative/Ablative	të	të

3. The "Definite Form", i.e. the form used <u>when directly following</u> a noun or nominal phrase in the Definite Form is as follows:

a. Singular

Case of preceding noun	Masculine	Feminine
Nominative	i	e
Accusative	e	e

	Genitive	i/e të	i/e së
	Dative/Ablative	të	së

b. Plural

Case of preceding noun	Masculine	Feminine
Nominative	e	e
Accusative	e	e
Genitive	i/e të	i/e të
Dative/Ablative	të	të

4. Articulated adjectives qualifying neuter nouns are preceded by clitics as follows:

Case of preceding noun	Definite	Indefinite
Nominative	e	i
Accusative	e	të
Genitive	i/e të	i/e të
Dative/Ablative	të	të

Examples are: **të kuqtë e madh**: *erysipelas*.

Unë dëshiroj ta harroj të ftohtët e vazhdueshëm: I *wish to forget the continuing cold weather*.

Kur të parit është i vështirësuar: *when vision is made difficult* (**Zëri**).

III   <u>USE OF "DEFINITE" FORMS</u>

1. As stated above, there are two forms of Adjectival/Genitive Clitic, described for convenience as the "Definite" and "Indefinite" forms.

2. The "Definite" form may be used only when the adjective or noun in the Genitive case directly follows a noun or nominal phrase in the Definite Form. Thus:

Shtetët e Bashkuara të Amerikës: *United States of America.*

Mundimet e kota të dashurisë: *Love's Labour's Lost.*

3. Before determining whether the "Definite" or "Indefinite" form is appropriate, the precise relationship between the nouns in a phrase has to be established. Compare:

Zyrtari i Ministrisë së Bujqesisë të Gjermanisë: *the official from the German Ministry of Agriculture.*

and:

Në periferinë e ndërtesës së Lidhjes së Prizrenit: *in the area around the building of the League of Prizren.*

and

Ngritja e ndërtesës së xhamisë së Kavajës: *the erection of the structure of the mosque of Kavaja.*

4. Third Declension masculine nouns such as **hoxhë** are followed by **i** in the Nominative case, but in the Oblique cases the Clitic **së** is used, as in:

Para shtëpisë së dajës së Valonit: *in front of Valon's uncle's house.*

And:

Zëdhënësi i Dukës së Madh (të Luksemburgut) :
the spokesman of the Grand Duke (of Luxemburg)
(Koha ditore).

5. Conversely feminine nouns (proper names) which belong to the First Declension such as **Antigon** and **Sadet** are followed by **e** in the Nominative and **të** in the Oblique cases.

6. Where an articulated noun is in one of the Oblique cases, and therefore preceded by the clitic **së**, any preceding Genitive Clitic following a feminine noun will be **të** rather than **së**, as in:

   ditëlindja e vajzës të së motrës: *the birthday of his sister's daughter.*

7. The particle **më**: *more*, used to form the Comparative and superlative forms of an adjective, is regarded as separating the adjective from the preceding noun, i.e. after **më** the Adjective Clitic will take the "Indefinite" Form.

PART D

NUMBERS

1. Cardinal nouns from zero to ten are as follows:

1. **një**		6. **gjashtë**	
2. **dy**		7. **shtatë**	
3. **tre/tri**		8. **tetë**	
4. **katër**		9. **nëntë**	
5. **pesë**		10. **dhjetë**	0. **zero**

2. They are all, except **zero** and **një**, followed by plural forms, and are generally followed by the Indefinite Form of the noun. **Një** will be followed by a plural when forming part of a larger number. They do not alter to denote the gender of a following noun in the Indefinite Form, except **tre**: *three*, which becomes **tri** before feminine nouns. They do not decline except when used as pronouns, or when used with **të** followed by a noun in the Definite Form, as in **të dyja shtetet**: *both states*. See below for details.

3. From 11-19 numbers are formed by agglutination, as in **katërmbëdhjetë**: *fourteen* (literally *four upon ten*).

4. **Njëzet**: *twenty* and **dyzet**: *forty* are formed by compounding on to the word **zet**, equivalent to the English *score*, but **zet** no longer exists independently. **Katërdhjetë** is frequently found in place of **dyzet**.

5. The other multiples of ten (30, and 50-90) are formed by compounding the two elements, as in **shtatëdhjetë**: *seventy*, and likewise multiples of 100.

6. All other numbers from 21 upwards are written as separate elements joined by **e**, as **njëzet e tetë**: *28*.

7. When cardinal numbers are used before nouns in the Definite Form, they are preceded by the Clitic **të** and if followed by a feminine noun take the ending -**a** or -**ja**, as in **të dyja, të tria, të katra**. However when the Clitic **të** is used to mean *all*, as in **të tridhjetë komunat e Kosovës**: *all thirty municipalities of Kosova*, the number does not take a feminine ending.

8. When used as pronouns 2 to 4 decline as follows:

	Masculine	Feminine
Nom./Acc.	**të dy**	**të dyja**
Oblique	**(i/e) të dyve**	**(i/e) të dyjave**

	Masculine	Feminine
Nom./Acc.	**të tre**	**të tria**
Oblique	**(i/e) të treve**	**(i/e) të triave**

	Masculine	Feminine
Nom./Acc.	**të katër**	**të katra**
Oblique	**(i/e) të katërve**	**(i/e) të katrave**

9. The ordinal numbers **i parë**, **i dytë**, etc. decline as normal adjectives. Ordinals from 3 to 5 (**i tretë**, **i katërt**, **i pestë**) and composite numbers based on them have separate forms, but ordinals from 6 to 9 are identical to the cardinal numbers. Composite numbers such as **tridhjetenëntë**: *thirty-ninth* are written as one word, omitting any final -**ë** before an **e**, and where *first* forms part of a composite number, as in **pesëdhjetenjëtë**: *fifty-first*, *first* is denoted by -**njëtë** rather than -**parë**.

10. Fractions are as follows:

gjysmë: *a half*, **një e trejta**: *one-third*, **çerek** or **një e katërta**: *one quarter*, **një e pesta**: *one fifth*. Although the numerator (e.g. 3 in ¾) is a number and therefore the denominator which follows should take the Indefinite Form, in practice it normally takes the Definite Form. Where it occurs in the Indefinite Form **një e katërt** is spelt without final **ë**, because the stress falls on the first syllable.

From **një e gjashta**: *one sixth* onwards the cardinal number, with the ending **-a** in place of **-ë**, is used as the denominator.

11. The suffix **-fish** (abbreviated from **fijsh**, Ablative Plural of **fill**) is used as a multiplier, as in **dyfish**: *double*, **gjashtëfish**: *sextuple*.

12. The suffix **-sh** is frequently used when referring to numbered objects, particularly when the number is represented by a figure. Readers of the Kosova press will be familiar with **A 4-shi** and **B 2-shi** (two of the blocks of the Obiliq power-station complex.)

13. The suffix **-she** is used to form nouns denoting objects of a certain quantity, such as **treshe**: *group of three*, **gjashtëshe**: *six-shooter* (revolver with barrel holding six rounds), **pesëdhjetëshe**: *fifty Lek note*.

14. **Dhjetë**, **qind** and **mijë** are invariable when used as numbers, either alone or prefixed by a multiplier, but when used to express an approximate quantity take the ending **-ra**. Examples of such use are:

Ramadan Muja ...rikujton kohët kur fshati kishte qindra shtëpi dhe mijëra banorë: *Ramadan Muja...recalls the times when the village* (Struzha) *had hundreds of houses and thousands of inhabitants* (**Koha ditore**).

Dhjetëra ushtarë të pagjetur: *tens (scores) of undiscovered soldiers* (Kadare, **Gjenerali i ushtrisë së vdekur**).

15. **Dhjetëra** and **qindra** are multipliers, and so in such expressions as **qindra mijë euro**: *hundreds of thousands of euros* the word *thousands* is grammatically a number.

16. Both **milion**: *million* and **miliard**: *milliard* (one thousand million) form the plural with **-ë** when used as numbers, but with **-a** to express quantities. Thus:

    Vetëm B-2-shi ka kushtuar rreth 60 milionë euro: *Just B-2 (Power Station) has cost 60 million euros (to repair)* (**Zëri**): and

    Kjo marrëdhënje, që i shkakton buxhetit të Kosovës humbje prej disa miliona eurove: *this agreement, which causes losses of millions of euros to the Kosova Budget.* (**Koha ditore**).

17. The confusion in the English-speaking world between the traditional (1 million million) and modern (1 thousand million) values of the billion is to some extent mirrored in Albanian. The following reflect the meanings shown in **Fjalor i shqipes së sotme**:

a. **Miliard** has the meaning *one thousand million*.

b. **Bilion** has the meanings *one thousand million* and *one thousand milliards* (i.e. one million million).

c. **Trilion** (plural **trilionë**) has the meaning *one thousand milliards* (i.e. one million million).

18. **Duzinë**: *dozen* is seen occasionally.

PART E

PREPOSITIONS AND NOMINAL PHRASES

1. Prepositions in Albanian can govern a variety of cases, and the case governed by each preposition is generally dependent on the type of preposition.

2. Prepositions are of three types, primary, secondary and compound. Compound prepositions are more accurately defined as prepositional phrases.

3. **Nga**: *from* or *towards*, its synonym **kah** and **te**: French *chez*, German *bei* (or **tek**, where euphony requires) can be regarded as primary prepositions. They govern the Nominative Case, and the following noun is always in the Definite Form unless the context specifically requires the Indefinite Form, as in:

    nga një tryezë tjetër, (Ismail Kadare, **Gjenerali i ushtrisë së vdekur**) contrasted with:

    Nga Universiteti i Tetovës: *from the University of Tetova.*

4. **Te** can be used to denote movement up to but not into, as well as location, as in:

    Ky kombibus shkon te Rrethi: *this minibus goes to* (the area near) *the Roundabout.*

5. Other primary prepositions are those such as **në**, **për** and **mbi** which are not recognisably derived from other words. Such prepositions generally govern the Accusative case and, except as set out below, may be followed by either the Definite or Indefinite Form.

6. After the prepositions listed below the following noun will be in the Indefinite Form unless it is qualified by an adjective or a following noun in the Genitive Case:

mbi, ndër, në, nën, nëpër, përmbi

Examples: **në qytet**: *in (the) town,* **nëpër luginë**: a*long the valley,* **në fshatin e madh**: *in the big village,* **në qendrën e qytetit**: *in the centre of (the) town.*

7.a After **në** place names are in the Indefinite Form, as in **në Shurdhan**: *in Shurdhan,* **në Pukë**: *in Puka,* even when qualified by an adjective or Genitive, as in:

në Banjë të Pejës: *in the village of Banja near Peja* (as opposed to villages elsewhere with the same name), **në Gllogjan të Deçanit**: *in the village of Gllogjan in the Deçan municipality,* **në Rogovë të Hasit**: *in Rogova in the Has area,* **në Davos të Zvicrës**: *in Davos in Switzerland.*

b. Where the first part of a geographical name is a common noun, it will be in the Definite Form, as in **në Malin e Zi**: *in Montenegro,* **në Luginën e Preshevës**: *in the Preshevë valley.* However, by analogy with the examples above, the forms **në Mal të Zi** and **në Luginë të Preshevës** are sometimes seen, and **në Han të Elezit**: *in Han i Elezit* prevails.

c. This applies to other proper nouns, as in (from **Zëri**):

Skënder Berisha-Kedi kthehet në Ramiz Sadik: *Skënder Berisha-Kedi rejoins the Ramiz Sadiku team.*

8. **Me**: *with* and **pa**: *without* are similar, but when used with a proper noun are followed by the Accusative Definite Form, as in **me Abdullahun**: *with Abdullah.*

9. **Më**: *on* can be used:

a. to specify dates or days, as in:

më 21 prill: *on 21st April*, **më të hënën**: *on Monday*.

b. (rarely) to indicate place as in:

më të dy anët: *on both sides*.

c. division, as in:

Palos më katërsh: *fold into four*.

10. Most secondary prepositions are followed by the Ablative Case. Secondary prepositions include:

afër: *near*, **buzë**: *close to*, **përballë**: *opposite*.

11. There are two prepositions which can be followed by either an Accusative or Ablative case:

a. **Ndaj** means *close to* when followed by the Accusative and *towards* when followed by the Ablative. However it is used with the Accusative only before a small number of articulated neuter nouns formed from participles as in the set expressions:

ndaj të gdhirë: *towards* (i.e. approaching, close to) *dawn* and **ndaj të ngrisur**: *towards dusk*.

b. **Për** means *for*, *about* when followed by the Accusative, and *by means of* when followed by the Ablative. It is used only with the indefinite Form of the Ablative, and primarily with parts of the body, as in **për dore**: *by hand*.

12. Many of the primary prepositions can be combined (sometimes spelt as one word, sometimes as two words) and the case following will depend on the second word or element.

13. The case governed by compound (phrasal) prepositions depends on the final word of the phrase. Thus:

a. Compound prepositions ending with **nga** will be followed by the Nominative Definite Form. Example:

për nga: *insofar as ....is concerned.*

b. Compound prepositions ending with **me** and other prepositions normally followed by the Accusative will be followed by the Accusative case. An example is:

Në lidhje me: *in connection with* (+ Accusative).

c. Where the final element of a compound preposition consists of a noun, the following noun will, subject to four exceptions, be in the Genitive case. Because the noun forming part of the preposition is in the Indefinite Form the following Clitic will always be **të** (except after **me anën**). Example: **Për shkak (të)**: *because of* (+ Genitive).

14. Four compound prepositions are followed by the Ablative. These are:

me anë, në bazë, në mes, për punë.

15. **Me anë** can be used with the Ablative, as above, and with the Clitic **të** followed by the Genitive. It must not be confused with **me anën**, which is followed by the Clitic **e** and the Genitive case.

PART F   READY REFERENCE LISTS AND
             TABLES

I   **MASCULINE NOUN-ENDINGS WITH REGULAR PLURAL FORMS**

1. This table shows the singular endings of the (masculine) nouns as classified in Part A, Section XV, together with those endings common to masculine and feminine nouns as listed in Part F Sections VI and VII. Against each ending is shown:

a. The regular plural (indefinite) form.

b. The plural Formation Class to which nouns with this ending belong.

c. Exceptions, individually if they are few, by reference to the relevant Paragraph of Section XV if numerous.

2. Where there is a significant number of exceptions, the symbol θ is used in the "Normal plural ending" column.

3. In the same column, where alternatives are shown, the first is the ending used for animate nouns, the second that used for inanimate nouns.

4. Where the same ending is found in both masculine and feminine nouns, the feminine ending is also shown.

5. Most animate nouns form the plural with **-ë**, many nouns denoting inanimate objects with **-a**, and most abstract nouns with **-e**. However these are observations rather than rules, and where no ending is shown a dictionary should be consulted.

CF Ending	Normal plural ending	Class No.	Exceptions/ Remarks/ Section
á	-llarë	13/16	A IX 6
ac	-ë	4	**daca**
aç	-ë	4	A XV 4: **-a** & **-e**
af	-ë	4	Exceptions in **-e**
ak	-ë	4	**leqe pleq ngjake merake** & **tiktake**: some Class 3
al	-ë / -e	6	**kuintalë dhaskenj**
am	-e	9	**kallama, xhama/xhame, gramë** and compounds and a few animate nouns
an	-ë θ	5	Five change **n** to **nj** (XV 5 g.): other exceptions **-a** & **-e**.
ant	-ë / -e	6	**altoparlantë** & **desantë**
aq	-ë	4	
ar	-ë θ	5	**barna/barëra**. Other exceptions **-e**:
as	-	1	Exceptions **-ë** & **-e**
ash	-ë	4	**desh gjeldasha** & some in **-e**
at	-ë / -e	6	Some Class 2: for others see A XV 6
az	-ë / -e	6	**shatërkaza**
azh	e	8	
e (Masculine)	-nj	12	Some Class 1, some with -rë
e (Feminine)		1F	
ec	-ë θ	5	**kotece**: **-a** for other exceptions
eç	-ë	4	**skeçe**
ek	-ë	4	**çeqe**: also A XV 3 z.
el	-ë / -e	6	Some inanimates in **-a, -ë**
en	-ë	4	**qen** & **bërshenj**: others in **-a** & **-e**

ent	-ë / -e	6	**centë precedentë**
er	-ë θ	5	**gjera**: others in **-e**
es	ë/e	-	See **-ues** and **-yes**
et	-ë / -e	6	**gërsheta koreta personalitete**
ez	-ë / -e	6	**diezë lezë breza**
ezh	-e	8	
ë (m.)	various	11	Mainly Classes 1 & 16
ë (f.)	-a	10F	Many in **-ë**, some in **-ëra**
ël (m.)	-e θ	10	Exceptions in **-e**
ël (f.)	-a	10F	
ëll (m.)	-e		See list in Part F
ëll (f.)	-a	10F	
ër (m.)	-a	10/1	**hatëre satëre talëre timbre**
ër (f.)	-a	10F	
ërr (m.)	-e	8	**vjehërr** Class 1
ërr (f.)	-a	10F	
i (First Declension)	-nj	12	Exceptions mostly **-rë**
i (Second Declension)	-nj	12	**mazi thi**
i (Feminine)	-	1F	Some 15F
id	-ë / -e	6	
ier/jer	-ë / -e	6	
ik	-ë	4	**armiq fiq miq** Several Class 3
il	-ë / -a θ	7	**bilbila, trishtila** and as listed at A XV 7
im	-e	8	**qilima trima** and animates in **-ë** as listed at A XV 8
in	-ë	4	**kaloshina puplina temina buletine kulmetinj**
ion	-e	8	As at A XV 8
ir	-ë θ	5	Exceptions **-e**

227

ist	-ë	4	ciste kiste shiste
it	-ë / -e	6	dolomitë meitë meteoritë satellitë shirita
ium	-e	8	
ok	-ë	4	doke: some Class 3
ol	-ë θ	5	Exceptions -a and -e
on	-ë θ	5	bulon kupon piston & napolon. and most -fon compounds take -a. Other exceptions take -e
ont	-ë / -e	6	
or	-ë θ	4	Exceptions in -e
osh	-ë	4	kosha lloshe/lloshra
ot	-ë	4	lot komplote mote
oz	-ë / -a	7	lloze
ozh	-e	8	
tar	-ë	4	
tor	-ë	4	
ua (m.)	-onj	13	kroje zgjoje përrenj
ues	-	1	
uk	-ë	4	shuka see also A XV 3 z.
ul (m.)	-a θ	10	Listed in Part F
ul (f.)	-a	10F	
ull (m.)	-uj	3	cullë, çulle, vrulle
ull (f.)	-a	10F	
um	-e	8	
un	-ë θ	5	barbunj: other exceptions -a & -e
ur (f.)	-a	10F	
ur (m.)	-ë θ		Listed in Part F
us	-e	8	autobusë mikrobusë obusë trolejbusë
yes	-	1	

II   **INFLECTIONAL VOWEL SUFFIXES**

1. This table deals only with suffixes and suffix endings, and not with stem endings.

2. As a suffix or suffix ending **a** can indicate:

    a. In nouns and preposed adjectives:

    i. Feminine Nominative Singular Definite.

    ii. Masculine Nom/Acc. Plural Indefinite.

    iii. Feminine Nom/Acc. Plural Indefinite.

    iv. Neuter Nom/Acc. Plural Indefinite.

    b. In adjectives:

    i. Feminine Plural.

    ii. Masculine Plural (e.g. **trima**).

    c. In pronouns and demonstratives:

    Masculine Plural.

3. As a suffix or suffix ending **e** can indicate:

    a. In nouns:

    i. Feminine Gen/Dat/Abl Singular Indefinite.

    ii. Feminine Nom/Acc. Plural Indefinite.

    iii. Feminine Nom/Acc Singular Indefinite.

iv. Nom/Acc Plural Indefinite of inanimate masculine nouns which become feminine in the plural.

b. In adjectives:

i. Feminine Singular.

ii. Feminine Plural.

4. As a suffix or suffix ending **ë** can indicate:

a. In nouns:

i. Masculine Nom/Acc. Singular Indefinite.

ii. Feminine Nom/Acc. Singular Indefinite.

iii. Neuter Nom/Acc. Singular Indefinite.

iv. Masculine Nom/Acc. Plural Indefinite.

v. Feminine Nom/Acc. Plural Indefinite.

b. In adjectives:

i. Feminine Singular.

ii. Masculine Plural.

5. As a suffix or suffix ending **i** and **u** can indicate in nouns:

a. Nom/Acc Singular Definite.

b. Gen/Dat/Abl Singular Indefinite.

6. As a suffix or suffix ending **o** can indicate:

   a. In (a very few) nouns: Masculine Nom/Acc. Plural Indefinite.

   b. In pronouns: Feminine Nom/Acc. Plural.

7. The following suffixes indicate Nom/Acc Plurals:

   a. Definite:

   -të indicates the Definite Plural of nouns ending in a stressed vowel or certain consonants (MPG/FPG 3 & 5).

   b. Indefinite:

   i. **-lerë**: Masculine nouns of Turkish origin.

   ii. **-llarë**: Masculine nouns of Turkish origin.

   iii. **-ra /-ëra**: mainly substance nouns.

III FEMININE NOUNS WITH MASCULINE DECLENSION

1. Proper names in long-standing use:

a. Ending in a consonant (of Arabic or Turkish origin):

Fiqret	**Ganimet**	**Idajet**	**Iqbal**
Irfan	**Iris**	**Kimet**	**Leman**
Mynever	**Nermin**	**Nimet**	**Sadet**

b. Ending in consonant or **-i** (of Greek origin):

Afroviti	**Andromaqi**	**Antigon**
Eleni	**Kaliopi**	**Ksanthipi**
Persefoni		

2. Names which in their original language end in or have variants ending in **-a**, such as *Ann (e)/Anna* have a CF ending in **-ë** and belong to the Third Declension, as do names derived from masculine names, such as **Xhuianë**: *Juliana*.

3. Other foreign names ending in a consonant such as **Sharon** and **Margaret** belong to the First Declension, thus.

   Isabeli zbutet në stuhi tropike: (*Hurricane*) *Isabel moderates to a tropical storm* (**Koha ditore**).

4. Names which after transliteration into Albanian end in **-i** such as **Meri** and **Hillari** also belong to the First Declension.

5. **Parzëm**: *bosom* declines as a masculine noun.

IV MASCULINE NOUNS WITH FEMININE DECLENSION

1. Proper names (a selection):

Dedë	**Kolë**	**Lekë**
Ramë	**Sulë**	**Tomë**
Çome	**Dule**	**Nile**
Aleko	**Deko**	**Foto**
Leo	**Niko**	**Spiro**

2. Nouns ending in -ë:

a. With plural identical to CF:

dukë	*duke*	**lalë**	*older person**
fëmijë	*child*	**papë**	*Pope*
gegë	*Gheg*	**toskë**	*Tosk*
judë	*Judas, betrayer*		

b. Forming plural with **-allarë**:

axhë	*uncle* (father's brother)
dajë	*uncle* (mother's brother)
hoxhë	*holy man, muezzin*

c. **Dajë** has alternative plural **daja**.

d. **Bacë:** *uncle* or *elder brother* forms plural **baca**.

3. Nouns ending in -e and -o:

qole	*servile person*
qose	*person without facial hair*
balo	*dog or ox with white-spotted face, rogue*
honxhobonxho	*charlatan**
kuqo	*redhead, red animal*
palaço	*clown*

4. **Zotëri:** *master* is masculine but declines as a Third Declension Group 4 noun.

5. The above lists contain the more commonly encountered nouns, and make no claim to be comprehensive.

V SELECTION OF "FALSE FRIENDS"

1. Nouns:

    The symbol ♠ indicates nouns which have a secondary meaning close to the English noun which they resemble.

afarist		*businessman*
agregat		*portable generator*
aktiv		*assets*
aranxhman		*package holiday*
armaturë		*framework (of building)*
azil		*old people's home*
bazëment	♠	*wheelbase*
central	♠	*(telephone) exchange*
dekor		*(useless) ornament*
diapason		*range, pitch, tuning-fork*
efektiv		*personnel*
ekspertizë	♠	*expert opinion*
ekspoziturë		*branch (of bank)*
ekonomist	♠	*book-keeper*
ekuivok		*misunderstanding*
evitim		*removal*
faktor	♠	*organisations (collectively)*
firmë	♠	*signature*
fraksion		*Parliamentary Faction, also grade (by grain size) of sand*
injorim		*disregard*
kamerier (e)		*waiter (waitress)*
kancelari	♠	*stationery, office*
komision	♠	*committee*
kompetencë		*responsibility, authority*
komunikacion	♠	*traffic*
kontingjent	♠	*shipment*
konvikt		*student hall of residence*

liferim		*delivery*
lokal (e)		*premises*
objekt	♠	*building*
opinion		*public opinion*
ordinancë		*clinic, medical or dental practice*
pallat	♠	*block of flats*
paralel	♠	*school class*
parolë		*banner*
patent	♠	*zip-fastener, driving licence*
perspektiv	♠	*prospect*
pjesëtar		*member*
relacion		1. *report* 2. *Road between A and B.*
situatë	♠	*Certificate*(for stage payments in building work)
spektër		*spectrum*
strukturë		*organisation*
subjekt	♠	*political party, organisation*
teknik		*technician*
televizion	♠	*TV station*
terrinë		*darkness*
tribunë		*lecture*
unifikim	♠	*homogenisation*
xhip/gjip		*Four-wheel drive vehicle*

2. Adjectives

adekuat	*appropriate*
i/e edukuar	*well brought up*
ekonomik	*business:* **hyrja ekonomike** = *service entrance*
kapital	*general, total*
konkret	*specific*
masiv	*mass, well-attended*
i/e shkolluar	*educated*
unik	*single, uniform*

VI FEMININE NOUNS ENDING IN -ËL, -ËLL, -ËN, -ËR, -ËRR, -ËZ, -UL, -ULL AND UR AND OTHER CONSONANT ENDINGS

1. These lists do not claim to be comprehensive.

2. Those nouns ending in **-ël**, **-ëll**, **-ën**, **-ër** and **-ërr** drop the **-ë** when the noun is inflected, as do some nouns ending in **-ëz**.

3. All nouns in these lists form the plural with **-a** except where otherwise stated.

4. Feminine nouns ending in **-ël**:

ashkël	*splinter*	**pikël**	*spot, drop*
bibël	*Bible*	**popël**	*boulder*
bokël	*corncob*	**pupël**	*feather, down*
bukël	*weasel**	**qingël**	*girth* (of horse)
buzël	*face veil*	**sigël**	*acronym*
cangël	*hook*	**stringël**	*trinket*
cefël	*rind, peel*	**thepël**	*splinter*
cifël	*splinter*	**thnegël**	*ant*
gogël	*berry, acorn*	**ubël**	*waterhole*
		vegël	*tool, instrument*
kërthingël	*lapwing*	**xhingël**	*trinket*
kokël	*lump**	**xhungël**	*jungle*
pantofël	*slipper*	**yçkël**	*trick, pretext*
petël	*petal*	**zogël**	*alder*

Dëngla: *eulogies** has acquired a derogatory meaning *prattle* and is found only in the plural.

5. Feminine noun ending in **-ëll**:

krikëll   *beermug*

6. Feminine noun ending in -**ëm**:

Parzëm: *chest, bosom* has Definite Form **parzmi**, plural **parzma**.

7. Feminine nouns ending in -**ën**:

gardhën	*groove for barrel-lid**	**lisën**	*thyme*
gomën	*deep place* (in water)	**mashën**	*see dictionary*
lekën	*female speckled trout*	**verzën**	*bilge*
		vregën	*flail*

8. Feminine nouns ending in -**ër**:

a. Forming plural with -**a**, as **femra**:

albër	*membrane**	**kodër**	*hill*
bushtër	*bitch* (canine)	**kryevepër**	*masterpiece*
çadër	*umbrella*	**kthetër**	*claw*
dhelpër	*fox*	**kuçedër**	*harpy*
femër	*woman*	**kudhër**	*anvil*
fibër	*fibre*	**kulpër**	*clematis*
flatër	*wing*	**lakër**	*cabbage*
flegër	*nostril*	**landër**	*oleander*
gatër	*sawmill*	**leskër**	*flake*
gënjeshtër	*lie*	**letër**	*paper*
glistër	*worm, parasite*	**lodër**	*toy*
gjëndër	*gland*	**lulelakër**	*cauliflower*
gjineshtër	*broom* (plant)	**lundër**	*boat*
hasër	*straw mat*	**mëngër**	*wooden trough*
hidër	*hydra*		
hudhër	*garlic*	**mitër**	*womb*
kadastër	*land registry*	**mjedër**	*raspberry*
kanistër	*basket*	**mjekër**	*beard*
kapistër	*halter*	**mokër**	*millstone*
katedër	*chair (academic)*	**mostër**	*sample*
		motër	*sister*

musëndër	*wall cupboard*	**shufër**	*rod*
ngastër	*plot (of land)**	**thadër**	*adze*
		thjeshtër	*step daughter*
palestër	*gymnasium*		
pudër	*powder*	**thembër**	*heel*
putër	*paw*	**thundër**	*hoof*
qendër	*centre*	**thupër**	*wand*
qiqër	*chickpea*	**ullastër**	*wild olive*
rriqër	*tick*	**vatër**	*home, hearth*
setër	*jacket*	**vedër**	*bucket*
skuadër	*squad*	**vepër**	*action, literary work*
sofër	*table*	**zebër**	*zebra*
shemër	*second wife*	**zemër**	*heart*
shënjestër	*sight*(of gun)	**zgavër**	*cavity*
shifër	*cipher*	**zhubër**	*crease*

b. The following do not have a plural form:

algjebër	*algebra*	**sedër**	*self pride*
kopër	*dill*	**thekër**	*rye*
lustër	*lustre**	**zëmër**	*afternoon tea*

c. **Thjeshtër** also means *stepson* and has both masculine and feminine declension forms. Likewise **shemër**, which means *rival* when masculine.

d. **Dhelpër** strictly speaking means *vixen*. **Skilak** denotes a dog-fox, and has a feminine counterpart **skile**. Both **skile** and **dhelpër** may describe a wily person.

e. As to place names, **Shkodër**, **Dibër**, **Çabër** and **Zhegër** are feminine. So too are **Zvicër**: *Switzerland*, **Akër**: *Accra*, **Londër**: *London*, **Flandër**: *Flanders* and **Sumatër**: *Sumatra*.

9. Feminine nouns ending in -ërr:

angërr	*hinge, cavity*	**gafërr**	*boulder*
		hikërr	*buck-wheat**
bokërr	*red field-mouse*	**kandërr**	*insect*
		kokërr	*grain*
çikërr	*sliver*	**puçërr**	*pimple*
dokërr	*limb bone*	**shkatërr**	*sting ray*
ëndërr	*dream*	**vjehërr**	*mother in-law*

Vjehërr also means *father-in-law* and has both masculine and feminine declension forms. **Vjehërri** means either *the in-law relationship* or *parents-in-law*.

10. Feminine nouns ending in -ëz:

These are nearly all diminutives, and are therefore not listed individually.

11. Feminine nouns with stems ending in -ul:

dheul	*ant*	**tumul**	*tumulus*
fabul	*fable*		

12. Feminine nouns with stems ending in -ull:

a. Forming plural in -a:

busull	*compass*	**nofull**	*jaw*
gotull	*creek*	**petull**	*pancake*
hatull	*structural timber**	**rregull**	*rule*
		pjergull	*pergola*
koçkull	*vetch*	**rregull**	*rule*
kukull	*doll*	**rrotull**	*circular or cylindrical object*
kumbull	*plum*		
mjegull	*fog*		
ndrikull	*bridesmaid**	**sqetull**	*armpit*

sumbull	*button, bud*	**tjegull**	*roof tile*
shpatull	*shoulder-blade**	**vetull**	*eyebrow*
shregull	*seesaw**	**vjedull**	*badger*

b. Without plural: **uthull**: *vinegar*.

13. Feminine nouns with stems ending in -**ur**:

    flutur   *butterfly*   **gjepur**   *poppycock*

14. The following nouns ending in other consonants are feminine:

Singular	Meaning	Plural
e diel	*Sunday*	**të diela**
gjanës	*braize* (fish)	**gjanësa**
lundërz	*otter*	**lundërza**
vatërz	*small strip of land*	**vatërza**

VII   MASCULINE NOUNS ENDING IN -ËL, -ËLL, -ËR, -ËRR, -ËZ, -UL, -ULL AND -UR

1. These lists do not claim to be comprehensive.

2. Nouns ending in -**ël**, -**ër**, and -**ërr** drop the -**ë** when the noun is inflected, subject to exceptions listed below. Those nouns ending in -**ëz** which are listed below retain the -**ë**, but some others (not listed) do not.

3. Except where otherwise stated, nouns listed here form the plural with -**a**.

4. Masculine nouns ending in -**ël**:

a. Forming plural in -**a**:

cingël	*peg, trinket*	**spektakël**	*spectacle*
monokël	*monocle*	**zegël**	*horsefly*

b. Forming plural in -**e**:

ansambël	*ensemble*	**triçikël**	*three-wheeled vehicle*
cikël	*cycle*		

5. Masculine nouns ending in -**ëll**:

gjasëll	*navelwort*	**hasëll**	*late planted pasture*

These two nouns do not drop the -**ë** in declension, and form the plural with -**e**: (**gjasëlle** and **hasëlle**).

6. Masculine nouns ending in -**ëm**:

a. Retaining the **ë** of the final syllable, and forming plural with **e**:

bakëm	*brazilwood*	**llagëm**	*drain*
kalldrëm	*cobbled pavement*	**takëm**	*set*

b. Dropping the **ë** of the final syllable:

i. Forming plural with -**a**:

Nouns ending in -**izëm**, and also **prizëm**: *prism*. In practice nouns ending in -**izëm** are nearly all abstract, and only a very few such as **aforizëm**: *aphorism*, **atavizëm**: *atavism*, **mekanizëm**: *mechanism*, and **organizëm**: *organism* have plural forms.

Examples: **aforizma**: *aphorisms*, **prizma**: *prisms*.

ii. Forming plural with **-e**:

istëm *isthmus* **ritëm** *rhythm*

Example: **ritme**: *rhythms*.

7. Masculine nouns ending in **-ër**:

a. The following drop the **-ë** when followed by an ending and form the plural with **-a**, as **libra**:

arbitër	*arbiter*	**krehër**	*comb*
cedër	*cedar*	**libër**	*book*
cilindër	*cylinder*	**ministër**	*minister*
cinxër	*cicada*	**misër**	*maize*
çafër	See dictionary	**numër**	*number*
		pjepër	*melon*
diametër	*diameter*	**pulovër**	*pullover*
dimër	*winter*	**qezër**	*eyetooth*
egjër	*chaff, tare*	**semestër**	*semester*
emër	*name*	**skafandër**	*diving-suit, space-suit*
filtër	*filter*		
frashër	*ash-tree*	**skeptër**	*sceptre*
kalibër	*calibre*	**spektër**	*spectrum*
ketër	*squirrel*	**tagër**	*tax*
kolibër	*humming-bird*	**tigër**	*tiger*
		urdhër	*command*

b. Compounds of **metër** are masculine and likewise form the plural by dropping the **ë** of the last syllable and adding **-a**; these include agent nouns such as **gjeometër**: *land surveyor*, nouns denoting instruments such as **barometër**: *barometer*, geometrical terms such as **diametër**: *diameter* and units of distance such as **centimetër** *centimetre* and **kilometër**: *kilometre*. Similarly multiples and fractions of **litër**.

c. **Kuadër**: *framework, personnel* forms plural **kuadro** and **teatër**: *theatre* forms plural **teatra** and **teatro**. **Kinoteatër**: *cinema/theatre* forms plural **kinoteatro**.

d. The following do not have a plural form:

ajër	*air*	**çumbër**	*spout*
alabastër	*alabaster*	**ekuilibër**	*equilibrium*
breshër	*hail*	**nishadër**	*sal ammoniac*
brigjër	*holly*	**prehër**	*lap, hem*
butër	*catarrh, glanders*		

e. The following drop the -ë of the final syllable when followed by an ending, but have a Nominative/Accusative Plural (Indefinite) form identical to the singular:

arbër	*Albanian living in Italy or Greece* *	**ftiziatër**	*TB specialist*
çoçër	*wren, dwarf*		
kumtër	*godfather*	**psikiatër**	*psychiatrist*
mjeshtër	*technician*	**shemër**	*rival*
pediatër	*paediatrician*	**vargër**	*breeding ram*

f. **Timbër**: *timbre* forms plural **timbre**.

g. **Hatër**: *favour*, **satër**: *meat cleaver* and **talër**: *open vat* retain the ë of the stem and form plural with -e.

Example: **hatëre**.

h. **Dhëndër**: *son in law* forms plural **dhëndurë**.

i. **Ohër** (both lake and town) is masculine, as is the river **Ibër**. So too is the river **Tigër**: *Tigris*.

8. Masculine nouns ending in **-ërr** (with plurals):

cërr	*wren*	**cërre**
kërr	*light-coloured horse, gray*	**kërre**
vjehërr	*father-in-law*	**vjehërr**

Cërr and **kërr**, being monosyllabic, retain the **ë** throughout their declension. **Vjehërr** drops the **ë** in all declined forms and has plural **vjehërr**.

9. Masculine nouns ending in **-ëz**: all those listed below retain the **ë** throughout their declension:

a. Forming plural in **-a**:

edepsëz *scoundrel** **mëz** *colt*

b. Forming plural in **-e**:

bëz *clod, dune* **çamçakëz** *chewing-gum, resin*

c. Forming plural in **-ë**:

hafëz *junior Muslim cleric*

10. Masculine nouns ending in **-ul**, all except **muskul** and **stimul** stressed on the last syllable:

a. Forming plural with **-ë**.

barxhul	*mottled goat*	**pezaul**	*small fishing-net*
çikul	*wicker*	**tërkul**	*pitchfork*
	snow-shoe	**veshul**	*bunch of grapes*
kanul	*spigot*	**xhaul**	*joule*

b. Forming plural with **-a**:

kaçul	*crest* (of plumage)	**sul**	*dugout boat*
trikul	*three pronged fork*		

c. Forming plural with **-e**:

ngul	*characteristic*	**shkul**	*skein**
pekul	*(see dictionary)*	**shul**	*post*
pezul	*ditch*	**tul**	*flesh, pith*
rul	*roller*		

Shul has alternative plural **shula**.

d. Forming plural with **-j**:

muskul	*muscle*	**stimul**	*stimulus*

e. A few nouns ending in **-ull** have alternative spellings ending in **-ul**.

11. Masculine nouns ending in **-ull**:

a. All these nouns form the plural with **-uj**:

akull	*ice*	**dishepull**	*disciple*
amull	*pond*	**fashikull**	*fascicle*
argull	*nit*	**frushkull/**	*whip*
artikull	*article*	**fshikull**	
avull	*steam*	**gadishull**	*peninsula*
barbull	*ball (of foot or thumb)*	**gamull**	*waterfall*
		gargull	*starling*
brambull	*marshy land*	**grehull**	*thicket*
brumbull	*humble bee*	**grumbull**	*mass*
cecull	*blacksmith's hammer*	**idhull**	*idol*
		ishull	*island*
cipull	*red fig, veil*	**kapitull**	*chapter*

245

konsull	*consul*	**skrupull**	*scruple*
kriskull	*sternum*	**strofull**	*lair*
kungull	*gourd*	**shakull**	*leather bottle*
matrikull	*register*	**shekull**	*century*
ndryshkull	*cypress*	**shembull**	*example*
orakull	*oracle*	**shpargull**	*asparagus*
popull	*people*	**shukull**	*pepperwort*
qefull	*mullet*	**tempull**	*temple*
qerthull	*winding reel*	**tingull**	*sound*
qipull	*gremlin*	**titull**	*title*
rrëqebull	*lynx*	**trangull**	*cucumber*
rrushkull	*butcher's broom **	**triskull**	*young sprout*
		trishull	*bladdernut*
rrobull	*(wood containing)* *Heldreich pine*	**turtull**	*turtle dove*
		zgarbull	*hollow* (in tree trunk)
rruzull	*globe*		

b. The following do not have a plural form:

    rrebull   *impetigo*   **rregull**   *rule*

c. **Cull**: *small boy, tot* forms plural **cullë**.

d. **Vrull**: *force, impetus* forms plural **vrulle**. Similarly **çull**: *horseblanket*.

12. Masculine nouns ending in **-ur** and **-aur**:

a. All masculine nouns ending in **-ur** except **hekur**, **lepur** and **pluhur** are stressed on the last syllable, although **flamur** may be stressed on either syllable. **Centaur** and **dinozaur** strictly speaking end in **-aur**, and have the stress on the first syllable of the final diphthong, while **kaur** is treated as a disyllabic word, i.e. the vowels **a** and **u** do not form a diphthong, and so the stress is on the **u**.

b. Forming plural with -ë:

abazhur	*sunblind*	**kaur**	*infidel*
centaur	*centaur*	**kontur**	*contour*
cimbur	*tick*	**lugur**	*curved knife*
dezhur	*person on duty*	**misur**	*bowl*
dinozaur	*dinosaur*	**pagur**	*water-canteen*
gur	*stone*	**silur**	*torpedo*
kangur	*kangaroo*	**ushkur**	*waistband*
karbur	*carbide*	**xhagajdur**	*braggart*

Hidrokarbur: *hydrocarbon* has plural **hidrokarbure**, and **qymyrgur**: *coal* has plural **qymyrgure**.

c. Forming plural with -e:

ahur	*cellar**	**kalambur**	*wordplay*
jodur	*iodide*	**klorur**	*chloride*
kusur	*change* (money)	**sulfur**	*sulphur*
mur	*wall*	**sur**	*facial feature*
ogur	*augury*		
qivur	*coffin*	**tambur**	*drum*

d. Forming plural with -a:

hekur	*iron*	**pluhur**	*dust*

e. **Bilur**: *porcelain* has no plural.

f. **Lepur**: *rabbit* forms plural **lepuj**.

g. **Flamur**: *flag* has alternative forms, depending on the stress used. The plural of **flámur** is **flámuj** whereas the plural of **flamúr** is **flamurë**.

VIII FEMININE NOUNS FORMING PLURAL WITH -ë

1. The following feminine nouns form the plural with -ë:

i. A small number of animate nouns:

bletë: *bee*, **kafshë**: *animal*, **lopë**: *cow*, **shtazë**: *animal* and **kumbarë**: *marriage witness*.

ii the following 101 inanimate nouns:

◊ indicates alternative plural with different meaning: see Class 17F.
♥ indicates noun with homonym ending in -a in plural.
♣ indicates alternative plural with same meaning.

algë ♥	*seed shell (of pine cone)*	**djersë**	*sweat*
anë	*side*	**enë**	*cooking pot*
armë	*weapon*	**fjalë**	*word*
barrë	*load*	**flakë**	*flame*
bathë	*horsebean**	**fletë**	*leaf*
besë	*pledge*	**gërshërë**	*scissors*
bimë	*plant*	**gojë**	*mouth*
bjeshkë	*Alpine pasture*	**gozhdë**	*nail*
botë	*world*	**gradë** ♥	*degree, rank**
brinjë ◊	*see 17F*	**groshë**	*bean*
bukë ◊	*see 17F*	**grykë** ◊	*see 17F*
buzë	*mouth*	**gjellë**	*meal, dish*
bythë	*backside*	**gjuhë**	*tongue**
cope ◊	*see 17F*	**gjurmë**	*trace*
dallgë	*wave*	**gjymtyrë**	*limb*
dardhë ♣	*pear*	**herë**	*time**
darë	*pincers*	**hundë**	*nose, beak*
degë	*branch*	**ijë**	*side, flank*
ditë	*day*	**javë**	*week*
		jetë	*life*

këmbë	leg*	plagë	wound
këmborë	clapper (of bell)	orë	fairy
		pakë	bacon lard
këmishë	shirt	palë ◊	see 17F
këngë	song	punë	work
këpucë	shoe	pushkë	rifle
klasë ♣	class	qepë	onion
kofshë	thigh	radhë	row, line
kokë ◊	see 17F	rangë	chores
kreshmë	fast	rragë	apron
lëkurë ◊	see 17F	rrënjë ♥	see below
lëndë	case, subject	rrugë	street
lëpjetë	dock, sorrel	sërë	row
lugë	spoon	sisë	udder, teat
llërë	upper arm	stinë	season
mangë	loafer	strehë	eaves
mëhallë	neighbourhood*	stromë	bedding
meshë	Mass	suvalë	breaker
mëngë	sleeve	shalë ♥	thigh
mollë	apple	shegë	pomegranate
munxë	expression of scorn	shkallë	ladder*
		shpesë	fowl
okë	see below	shpezë	bird
orë	hour	tragë	track
pendë	feather*	trazë	spit
petë ◊	see 17F	thekë	stamen
pëllëmbë	palm (of hand)	udhë	way
pikë ◊	see 17F	urë ♥	firebrand
pjesë	part	vegjë	loom
pashkë	Easter	vezë	egg
pemë	fruit-tree	vojvodë	see dictionary
pjeshkë	peach	zorrë	intestine

2. This list was compiled from **Fjalori i shqipes së sotme**.

IX   PREPOSITIONS AND CASES GOVERNED

1. The following prepositions require the Nominative case and the Definite Form, but the Indefinite Form may be used if the context requires:

    nga and its synonym **kah**: *from, towards**, **te** (or **tek**): *at* or *to the location of* (Approximate equivalents to **te** are French *chez* and German *bei*).

2. The following prepositions require the Accusative case and the Indefinite Form, unless the noun governed is qualified by an adjective or a following noun in the Genitive case, in which case the Definite Accusative is used:

    mbi: *over*, **në**: *in, to*, **përmbi**: *over, above, in addition to*.

    Place-names following **në** remain in the Indefinite Form, even when qualified by an adjective. See Part E.

3. **Me**: *with* and **pa**: *without* are normally followed by the Indefinite Accusative, unless the noun is qualified (as above), but a following proper noun will take the Definite Form.

4. The following prepositions require the Accusative:

deri	*as far as*	**nën**	*under*
gjer	*until*	**nëpër**	*through,*
më	*on* (date)		*along*
ndër	*among*	**që, qysh**	*since*

5. **Ndaj** and **për** may both be used with either the Accusative or Ablative.

a. **Ndaj**: *towards* is used before the Accusative only with nouns derived from participles (i.e. Gerunds), in expressions such as:

ndaj të gdhirë: *towards* (i.e. approaching, close to) *dawn* and **ndaj të ngrisur**: *towards dusk*.

When used before the Ablative it means *towards*.

b. **Për** means *for, about* when followed by the Accusative, and *by means of* when followed by the Ablative.

6. The following prepositions require the Ablative:

afër	*near*	**kundër**	*against*
anës	*along*	**larg**	*far from*
ballë	*opposite*	**lart**	*above*
brenda	*inside*	**matanë**	*on the other side*
bri	*beside*		
buzë	*by, near*	**mbas/pas**	*after*
drejt	*towards*	**mes/midis**	*between*
gjatë	*during*	**ndërmjet**	*among*
jashtë	*out of*	**para**	*in front of*
krahas	*alongside*	**përpjetë**	*up*
pos/veç	*except*	**rrëzë**	*at the foot of*
poshtë	*down*	**sipas**	*according to*
pranë	*near to*		
prapa	*behind*	**sipër**	*above*
prej	*from*	**tat përjetë**	*down*
qark/rreth	*around*	**tej/tutje**	*beyond*

7. Most phrasal prepositions are followed by the Genitive, unless the last element is itself a preposition, when that preposition will take its normal case.

8. The following phrasal prepositions are followed by the Ablative: **me anë, në bazë, në mes, për punë**.

X **FAMILY TREE**

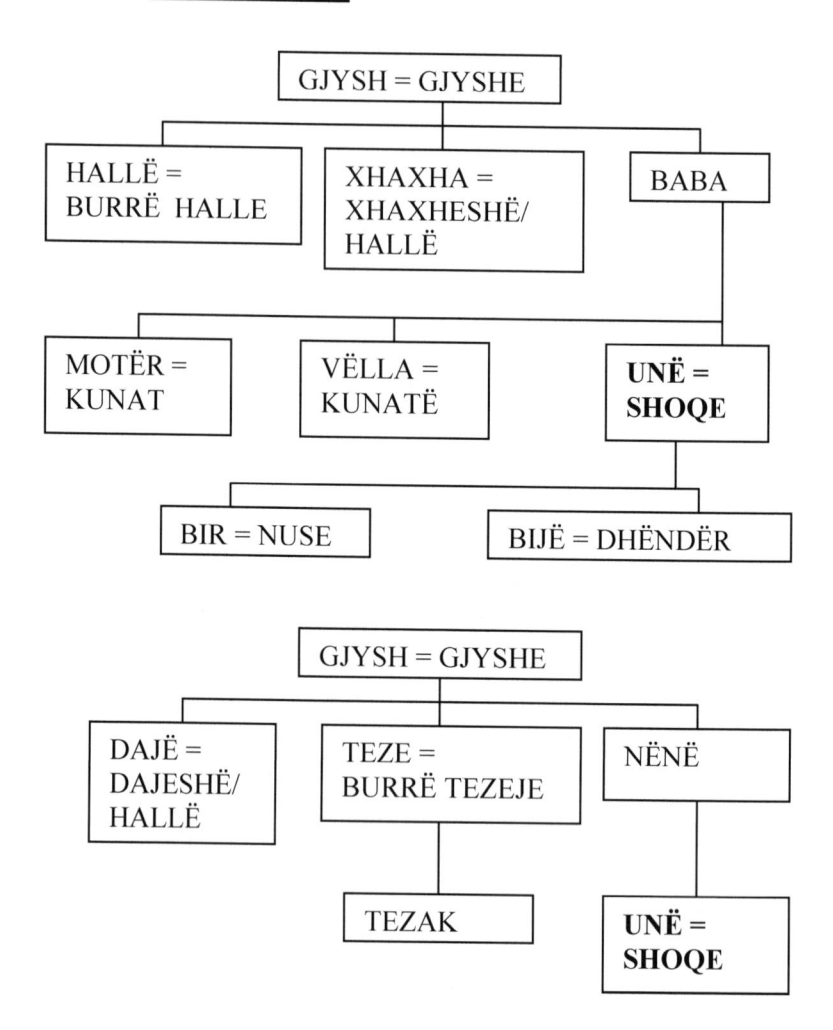

```
                    GJYSH = GJYSHE
           ┌───────────────┼───────────────┐
     HALLË =         XHAXHA =            BABA
     BURRË HALLE     XHAXHESHË/           │
                     HALLË                │
           ┌───────────────┼───────────────┐
       MOTËR =         VËLLA =          UNË =
       KUNAT           KUNATË           SHOQE
                                          │
                              ┌───────────┴──────────┐
                         BIR = NUSE            BIJË = DHËNDËR
```

```
                    GJYSH = GJYSHE
           ┌───────────────┼───────────────┐
       DAJË =           TEZE =            NËNË
       DAJESHË/         BURRË TEZEJE        │
       HALLË                │               │
                          TEZAK          UNË =
                                          SHOQE
```

THE END

252